Make an Interactive Science Museum

Hands-on exhibits

Robert Gardner

Illustrations by Kris Kozak

TAB Books

Imprint of McGraw-Hill

New York San Francisco Washington, D.C. Auckland Bogotá
Caracas Lisbon London Madrid Mexico City Milan
Montreal New Delhi San Juan Singapore
Sydney Tokyo Toronto

McGraw-Hill

*A Division of The **McGraw·Hill** Companies*

pbk   1 2 3 4 5 6 7 8 9 BBC/BBC 9 0 0 9 8 7 6 5

Library of Congress Cataloging-in-Publication Data

Gardner, Robert, 1929-
   Make an interactive science museum / by Robert Gardner.
      p.   cm.
   Includes index.
   Summary : Provides instructions which enable students and teachers
to build their own science museums in places where the exhibits can
be seen on a regular basis.
   ISBN 0-07-022866-3 (H). — ISBN 0-07-022867-1 (P)
   1. Science museums—Exhibitions—Design and construction—Juvenile
literature.   2. Science museums—Educational aspects—Juvenile
literature. [1. Science projects.   2. Museums.   3. Exhibitions.]
I. Title.
Q105.A1G37   1995
507'.5—dc20   95-22078
                                                          CIP
                                                          AC

Acquisitions editor: Kimberly Tabor
Editorial team: Lori Flaherty, Managing editor
            Joanne Slike, Executive editor
            Alfred B. Bortz, Ph.D., Duquesne University School of Education,
            Technical reviewer
Production team: Katherine G. Brown, Director
            Donna K. Harlacher, Coding
            Janice Ridenour, Computer artist
            Brenda M. Plasterer, Desktop operator
            Nancy K. Mickley, Proofreader
            Joann Woy, Indexer
Design team: Jaclyn J. Boone, Designer
            Katherine Lukaszewicz, Associate designer   AN2
            Kris Kozak, Illustrator   0228671

Contents

Part 3
Interactive exhibits   43

Part 4
Optical mysteries and other puzzles   77

Preface

AFTER more than 35 years of teaching science, I came to realize that the science exhibits I prepared to generate interest among students and other teachers was one of the most rewarding things I did. The exhibits were fun to prepare, and they often generated insightful questions and interesting discussions. The greatest rewards were when students asked if they could prepare a display. Those students who prepared exhibits most likely learned more in building their displays than they ever learned in my classroom. Consequently, my experiences in this phase of education led me to write this book.

Science museums with hands-on exhibits have generated interest, excitement, and enthusiasm for science in many young people. Visiting a science museum is a lot of fun, but few of us can visit exhibits frequently or even on a regular basis. The purpose of this book is to enable students and teachers to build their own science museums in places where the materials displayed can be seen on a daily or regular basis. Such museums, even if they consist of a single exciting exhibit, can help arouse an enthusiasm for science. Building exhibits is also a good way to learn about science, because in order to prepare a meaningful and effective display, you must understand the idea or principle that it is designed to explain.

If there is sufficient space to develop a number of exhibits in your small museum, you might decide that a group effort is needed. The opportunity to work with others enables you to learn from them as they learn from you. Group efforts also provide valuable experience in working closely with other people who share a common interest.

Introduction

MAKE an Interactive Science Museum contains a great variety of exhibits on such subjects as electricity, light and shadows, lenses, images, mirrors, the human body, music, art, evaporation, plants, seeds, insects, rocks, astronomy, water and other liquids, animals and animal tracks, and more. Almost every area of science is represented.

Each exhibit includes a list of materials you'll need to build the exhibit, a brief explanation of what the exhibit should demonstrate or teach, and suggestions on how to display your exhibit and the type of questions or information you might provide visitors.

Exhibits are grouped into hands-on exhibits, puzzles to ponder and mysteries to figure out, ongoing exhibits that can be watched daily, exhibits for thoughtful viewing, and exhibits that demonstrate a scientific principle.

Part 1 describes how to plan and build exhibits, where you might build your museum, and how you might best display materials so as to attract visitors to your museum.

Part 2 contains hands-on exhibits where museum visitors can *do* something with materials rather than just observing and reading about them.

Part 3 contains more hands-on exhibits but with an added dimension. These exhibits require your museum visitors to perform actions within an experiment. The actions performed lead visitors to the answer, to a question, or to the discovery of a pattern or law of nature.

Part 4 contains exhibits on puzzles, illusions, and mind teasers. You might find that some of the exhibits in this section are the most popular in your museum! Puzzles encourage people to use their analytical abilities, test their senses, and challenge their ideas.

The exhibits in Part 5 contain living and nonliving materials that undergo change. They are "eyes-on" exhibits rather than hands-on exhibits and are most appropriate in a museum setting where people can and do return on a regular basis.

Part 6 contains exhibits that are best displayed as things to see rather than touch. Their shape, color, structure, or other features make them interesting and attractive to museum visitors. Some exhibits illustrate a scientific principle or concept as well as the art aspects. Visitors will be asked to make careful observations of materials, although they will not be actively involved in manipulating the exhibits.

Make an Interactive Science Museum contains more exhibits than you will have time to put together. Consequently, work on those exhibits that spark your enthusiasm to create displays, experiments, demonstrations, puzzles, or mysteries that others can enjoy and learn from. Don't hesitate to design, develop, and build your own displays, however. You might already have some ideas you would like to bring to the attention of others. As you work on displays and exhibits, you might discover a variation to or a totally new approach to presenting a fundamental scientific principle. If you do, pursue it. Working on your own ideas is always more fun than working on someone else's.

Although this book is written for a young audience, teachers will find it to be a rich source of ideas. Most classrooms have space for one or two exhibits, and if your museum extends into hallways, libraries, and other classes, it might generate schoolwide enthusiasm for science and learning.

Finally, your museum need not be limited to science. You will find some math-, music-, and art-related exhibits within these pages, and exhibits involving history, English, social studies, and other disciplines can be included in your museum as well.

How to use this book

What the ⚠ symbol means

Most of the exhibits in this book you can do yourself. However, there are some exhibits that require the use of electrical power tools, sharp scissors, or materials that must be used with caution. Whenever you see the safety icon ⚠, you need to find an adult to assist you. A teacher, parent, or other adult can determine what parts of the project you can perform without supervision and which parts you should only do with their help.

Safety is important; use good judgment and find an adult to help you whenever you see the ⚠ symbol.

Metric and English units

Authors and publishers frequently include both English and metric units, usually with one in parentheses, when readers are asked to take measurements or purchase material. In this book, I have used the units most commonly used for the measurement in question and have not included other units in parentheses. For example, lumberyards in the United States use English units. They sell 2×4s, and it is understood that they are selling boards that are 2 inches by 4 inches. On the other hand, chemists and druggists usually measure volumes in milliliters or liters—small volumes in milliliters (mL) and large volumes in liters (L). If for any reason, you feel the need to use a unit other than the one given, refer to the metric conversion table at the end of the book.

Part 1

Introduction to science museums and exhibits

MUSEUMS have been around for a long time, but they have changed dramatically in the last several hundred years. The word *museum* comes from the Greek word *mouseion*, which was a building sacred to the muses where people left offerings. The muses were the nine goddesses of the arts and sciences worshipped by many early Greeks.

Early museums

One of the earliest museums was in Alexandria, Egypt. It was founded in the third century B.C. and served as a university for scholars. During the seven centuries that it existed, its curators preserved statues of prominent scholars, astronomical and surgical instruments, tusks recovered from elephants, the skins of rare animals, and a variety of other objects presented as gifts and offerings.

During the Middle Ages, European churches, monasteries, and universities collected scholarly manuscripts and relics. A few wealthy noblemen and royal families established private collections of art, gems, jewelry, relics, and a variety of other valuables, but ordinary people had no opportunity to enter these "museums." In fact, the royal collections at the Louvre in Paris were not opened to the public until after the French Revolution.

In America, museums were generally more democratic. One of the first public museums in the new world was the Charleston Museum in Charleston, South Carolina, which was established in 1773. During the 1840s, gifts to the United States government from James Smithson, an English chemist, gave rise to the Smithsonian Institution, which continues to this day.

By the twentieth century, museums were springing up in every major city in the country. The purpose of these institutions was to make collections, exhibits, and displays available to the public. Museums were no longer for the elite; they were open to everyone. Many citizens with little formal schooling educated themselves by reading and by spending their free time at museums.

Today, in addition to traditional museums, popular traveling exhibits move from museum to museum or from school to school. Inside modern museums, educational programs and hands-on exhibits have become increasingly common. Instead of being told to "Keep Hands Off," we more commonly see signs that say "Please Touch" or that tell us how to go about manipulating the objects found in an exhibit. The attraction for most people to some of the exhibits that you will build in your own science museum will probably be the hands-on materials. That is why so much of this book is devoted to those activities.

Creating your own museum

When you hear the word *museum*, you might think of a big spacious building with lots of exhibits, but a museum can also be a corner in a room where an exhibit or an activity is set up. If people can go to the corner and learn something, either by looking and reading or by engaging in a hands-on experiment, then the corner exhibit is every bit as valuable as a similar exhibit surrounded by glass and located between marble pillars in a large city museum.

The point is that a museum can occupy a large space or a small one. It can fill an entire room in your house or school, one side of a hallway outside your classroom, one wall in the foyer of a library or other town building, a portion of a playground or lawn, or a corner of your family's living room. What is important is the content or potential for learning offered by the exhibit. Of course, many various worthwhile exhibits make for a more interesting museum and will engage visitors for longer periods.

Every museum has a *curator*, the person who oversees the exhibits and is in charge of the museum. If you like to make things, enjoy helping others learn, and find science interesting, you could be a good curator for your own small science museum. However, you don't have to do everything yourself. Your classmates or siblings might be interested in establishing a small museum too. You might even convince your teacher, librarian, parent, a store owner, or a town official to help you organize or plan the science museum. These people might even help you find space and materials for your exhibits.

Types of exhibits

You can't build a successful science museum unless you have exhibits that people will enjoy seeing, studying, or manipulating. The exhibits can take on a variety of forms and formats. You could have hands-on experiments that require people to do things with materials that use batteries, bulbs, and switches, for example, or you could have hands-on demonstrations in which the observer carries out some simple manipulation and then watches the result. Other types of demonstrations could be automatic, providing enough visible evidence so that people can simply read a brief description of the exhibit and then watch to see what happens. Your museum could have puzzles to ponder or manipulate; ongoing events to be observed over time, such as the germination of seeds or the growth of mold; or exhibits with short explanations that are viewed for their beauty or the interest they generate. The possibilities are unlimited. All it takes is interest, imagination, enthusiasm, and energy.

You will find plenty of suggestions for exhibits in this book, but you need not feel restricted to the ones described here. You might be able to think of and build exhibits that are more interesting to you than any about which you read. Upon preparing one or more of the suggested exhibits, you might also discover extensions, modifications, or additional activities that you want to pursue. By all means do so, but check with a knowledgeable adult before you attempt to build or use anything that could be dangerous. Again, remember that suggested exhibits in this book that require adult supervision or special precautions are noted with the *caution* icon ⚠ .

Planning your museum

Once you decide to build your own science museum, you need to begin planning. One of the first things you have to decide is whether you want to work alone or with a group.

If your museum is to be a small one, along a wall or a corner of the family living room, it makes sense to work alone or with the help of family members. On the other hand, if you plan to have exhibits along the corridor of a school, you might want to ask a few of your classmates to help you design and build the exhibits, as well as a teacher to serve as a consultant.

If the museum is a class project involving a number of people, you have to work together in a cooperative manner if the project is to succeed. The group might choose to elect leaders or your teacher might serve as a project director.

As well as deciding what exhibits to build, you must spend some time planning how the work is to be divided and scheduled before you actually begin to construct the exhibits. You should remember that everyone participating in the museum project has a right to speak and to be heard. Ideas that seem crazy at first might prove to have merit when considered in detail, seen as full-fledged exhibits, or modified in group discussion.

Estimating space and planning layout

Before you choose your exhibits, you need to find out what space is available. Does the space lend itself to displaying exhibits in terms of lighting, electrical outlets, and configuration? What equipment is available to house and display the exhibits? Many schools and libraries have glass-covered display cabinets, tables, and shelves that you can use, but are these items suitable for what you plan to display on them? Evaluate the proposed exhibits and determine if they are possible given the space and materials available. If not, can the space and facilities be changed to accommodate the exhibits?

You also need to consider how to best organize the museum. How can the various exhibits best be arranged? Placing exhibits with a similar theme near one another makes sense. If exhibit two cannot be understood without the information provided in exhibit one, then people visiting the museum should be made aware of that fact. If possible, the exhibits should be arranged so that visitors see exhibit one before exhibit two.

Some of the proposed exhibits might be more effective if combined. In this case, the people responsible should work together in organizing, setting up, and displaying the materials.

Before you begin to place exhibits, you'll need to estimate the space required for your or your group's work. This can be done by making a scale drawing that includes the overall dimensions of the exhibit. Once the space has been divided up among the exhibitors, a more detailed plan can be prepared. The detailed plan should include the size and placement of drawings, pictures, photographs, charts, graphs, words, and materials that are to make up the displays.

Materials and costs

If the school, library, or other building where the museum is to be located has display cabinets, cases, or shelves, you should try to make use of them. If such space is being made available to you, it is probably because it is not being used to its best advantage at the present time. The person or persons responsible for these display areas are hoping you can bring them to life. Try not to disappoint them.

It is not likely that you can afford to buy museum-quality display units. However, if you or someone in your group is skillful with wood, you might be able to make shelves, cases, and cabinets for your exhibits. If not, you might know an adult with such skills who would be willing to help you. A builder might provide you with scrap lumber left over from a job if you ask for it. A lumberyard might offer to give you broken or poor quality lumber that they can't sell. Second-hand stores or thrift shops are also a good source of furniture, lights, or other materials that you could use. An adult might help you scrounge useful lumber, furniture, or other items from a landfill, transfer station, or recycling center.

Many hands-on experiments and demonstrations can be set up on small tables or counters. If dim light is required, you might have to build a simple enclosure using dark cloth hung from wires or curtain rods. Large pieces of cardboard can be scored and bent or taped together and placed on a table to make a background for exhibits. The cardboard can also be used as a place to hang, glue, tape, or tack pictures, photographs, drawings, charts, and printed materials. You might also use thin plywood, chipboard, pegboard, bulletin boards, and other materials. Pegboard is particularly useful for hanging pictures. The pegs can be moved easily from place to place until you have the pictures arranged in the most attractive way possible for your exhibit.

For hands-on exhibits, avoid using anything that could be dangerous to visitors or animals. Also, do not leave valuable materials where they are accessible to those visiting your exhibit. They might disappear when you are not nearby.

Many of the materials you will need to build exhibits can be found in local lumber, hardware, grocery, and drug stores. Less readily available items such as battery holders, sockets for small flashlight-size bulbs, magnets, switches, insulated wire, alligator clips, and so on are probably stocked by your school. If not, you can probably purchase them at an electronics store or through a science supply house (see Resources). Your teacher will probably have catalogs for one or more of these supply houses.

Displaying exhibits

You will want your exhibits to be as appealing as possible. Photographs and drawings, either your own or those found in books and magazines, can help to enhance and explain an exhibit. Drawings can be easily enlarged by most modern copiers. Even colored photographs can be copied and enlarged if you have access to a copier that can reproduce color. If you have artistic talent, you might prepare your own paintings to add interest and beauty to an exhibit. Diagrams and charts are useful in developing good explanations of exhibits, hands-on experiments, or demonstrations.

All visual aids created to increase understanding should provide enough contrast and size so that they can be easily seen or read by those who visit your museum. Black on white provides the most common, easily seen contrast, but other contrasting colors such as red on green, silver on black, or gold on blue, can add "zip" to a display. Generally, colorful materials make an exhibit more attractive and draw people to it. However, visitors will not stay unless the content is appealing, interesting, and of substance.

Print, type, or word process all the words that are to appear at your exhibit. Be sure to check your spelling and grammar before you actually post any printed material in your display area. Have someone who is a good speller and grammarian edit the written part of the exhibit. If you have a word processing program that checks spelling, be sure to use it. Misspelled words detract from any exhibit regardless of how good the actual content is.

Try to find an attention-getting title for your exhibit. If you have developed an experiment to show how colored lights can be mixed to form new colors, you might use "Mixing Colors" as a title. However, a title such as "The Secrets of Mixing Colored Lights" will probably attract more people to the exhibit. Because people like to know about secrets, the title will attract them even if they are color-blind.

Avoid trying to do too much with a single exhibit. Focus on a single idea, story, experiment, or demonstration. Try to prepare several exhibits based on a single theme, each dealing with one fundamental principle, rather than trying to include all the principles in one exhibit. The main object or objects in your exhibit should be near its center. You can use arrows or other ways to bring the viewer's vision to the main point of the exhibit. Ribbons or wires leading from print to objects, photos of people pointing, or animals leaping can all be used to draw attention toward the principal part of the exhibit. Numbers and arrows can be used to lead the viewer along the logical sequence of ideas in an exhibit. Try to keep the words that accompany your exhibit easy to read and few in number. If possible, let objects rather than words carry the message you want to convey.

A display should have balance and proper proportion. Try not to have all the equipment or objects of primary interest on one side. If possible, arrange the viewing of the exhibit materials in a series of rectangles. Greek artists and mathematicians discovered what is known as the golden ratio. They found that a rectangle with sides having a ratio of 1.618:1 was the most appealing to view. A ratio of 8:5 is a very close approximation to the golden ratio, but any reasonably similar ratio such as 5:3, 7:4, 3:2, and so on are more appealing than squares or long thin rectangles.

If you do not have access to a computer and you have difficulty lettering by hand, you can buy stencils or precut letters at stationery or art stores that enable you to provide lettering that looks quite professional. A zero-cost approach is to cut large, colored letters or words from magazines and carefully paste them onto heavy paper or poster board.

Specialize or generalize

Unless you plan to offer one long-lasting exhibit, you have to decide whether your museum is going to concentrate on one area of science, such as light, electricity, plants, and animals, or whether it is going to provide information about several areas of science, such as chemistry, physics, biology, geology, ecology, entomology, and so on. If the museum is the project of a single class, then specializing in whatever topic the class is studying is a reasonable approach. If the museum is made up of exhibits that stem from projects carried out by different people, then the exhibits will reflect the varied interests of the participants.

Extensions of the museum

An exhibit developed for the museum might very well serve as a science fair project or a science class assignment. Certain exhibits might become part of a mobile museum, which is a museum on wheels. For a mobile museum, the exhibits are mounted on carts, carried on tables, or easily moved in boxes from classroom to classroom or to another school, a local library, a nursing home, a day-care center, town offices, local stores, hospitals, offices, and waiting rooms. In this way, the exhibits and the information they convey can reach a wider audience.

Part 2

Hands-on exhibits

Hands-on exhibits are generally the most popular type of exhibits. Most people prefer to do something with materials rather than just observing and reading about them. If you decide to set up hands-on exhibits, you need to periodically change them, particularly if the patrons of your museum are frequent visitors. For example, if your museum is located in a classroom or a school corridor, students and teachers are able to view the exhibits every day that school is in session. In such a situation, changing any hands-on exhibits at least once a week makes sense. Otherwise, patrons will lose interest and your exhibits will be ignored, which destroys the very purpose of a viable museum.

About half the exhibits described in this chapter are related to electricity—an always popular topic—culminating in the construction of an electric quiz board. Once you have built the quiz board, it can be used in a variety of other exhibits.

In addition to electrical exhibits, information is included to help you design and build exhibits that allow your patrons to enjoy hands-on experience with pinhole images, colorful giant soap films, fingerprints, making estimates, and seeing what they know to be a million objects all in one place. The end of the chapter contains a list of ideas for additional exhibits that you might like to pursue and develop on your own. Now, let's explore some exhibits beginning with one called "The Oersted effect."

The Oersted effect

In the winter of 1819 to 1820, Hans Christian Oersted, quite by accident, made a startling discovery, one that showed for the first time that electricity and magnetism are related. You can prepare a hands-on demonstration that allows those who visit your museum to see the same effect that brought fame to Oersted nearly two centuries ago.

Materials

- ➤ 2 PVC-insulated copper wires, one appx. 6 inches long; the other appx. 4 feet long
- ➤ wire cutter
- ➤ tape
- ➤ 2-foot-long board, appx. 4 inches wide
- ➤ modeling clay
- ➤ 2 magnetic compasses
- ➤ 6-volt, dry-cell battery
- ➤ metal thumbtack
- ➤ table, low shelf, or counter

Use the wire cutter to strip approximately 1 inch of insulation from the ends of both wires. Place the long wire in the center of the board. Affix one of the compasses to the board with clay so that it is above the wire. Affix the second compass to the board so it is beneath the long wire. Be sure the compass needles are parallel to the wire (Fig. 2-1). Tape the wire in place, and attach one end of the long wire to one pole of the battery. Push the tack into the board at one end of the board and wrap the wire under the head of the tack. Affix the other end of the 6-inch-long wire to the other pole of the battery. The other end of the shorter wire should be free.

Figure 2-1

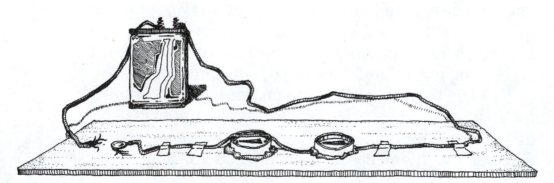

The instructions to those visiting this exhibit at your museum might read as follows:

Watch the two compass needles as you touch the bare end of the short wire to the head of the tack in the board. What happens to the compass needles when current flows through the wire? *Don't connect the wire to the tack for more than a few seconds.* Prolonged connections will wear out the battery.

You've just seen what Oersted saw in 1819. At that time, everyone thought electricity and magnetism were totally unrelated. Oersted's accidental observation provided the first clear evidence that magnetism and electricity are related. As Louis Pasteur later noted, "In the field of experimentation, accident favors the prepared mind." Because Oersted was interested in the similarities between electricity and magnetism, he recognized the significance of an observation that others had probably made but ignored.

Why do you think the two compass needles turned in opposite directions? (Answer: The magnetic field above the wire has the opposite direction of the field beneath the wire.)

Other people saw the same effect and paid no attention to it. Why do you think they ignored it ? (Answer: They didn't believe that electricity and magnetism were related.)

Conductors and nonconductors

An electric charge can move through some materials and not through others. Those substances through which a charge moves are called *electrical conductors*, and the flowing charge is called an *electric current*. Substances through which current does not move are called *nonconductors* or *insulators*. Some substances, such as arsenic and germanium, conduct a charge, but far less readily than true conductors. Such substances are appropriately called *semiconductors*.

In this exhibit, visitors at your museum can test a number of different materials for conductivity. They do this by touching the ends of two wires to the opposite ends of the material being tested. If the substance is a conductor, a bulb lights; if it is a nonconductor, the bulb does not light.

Materials

> ➤ large board or tabletop
> ➤ transparent tape
> ➤ 2 flashlight bulbs
> ➤ light bulb socket to fit one of the flashlight bulbs
> ➤ 1–15 items made of different substances
> ➤ 2 D-cell batteries
> ➤ battery holder for D-cell batteries
> ➤ 2 PVC-insulated wires appx. 1 foot long, each with an alligator clip on one end
> ➤ 1 PVC-insulated wire appx. 6 inches long
> ➤ self-adhesive labels (optional)

Tape the different items you've collected to a large board or tabletop (Fig. 2-2). You might include such things as a nail, a coin, a table knife or spoon, a rubber band, a piece of chalk, a pencil, a candle, a glass rod or tube, a piece of plastic, cardboard, pencil lead, wires, cloth, paper, and so on. Also, tape one of the flashlight bulbs to the board or tabletop. Stick-on labels can be placed beside items that might not be recognized. Remember to check the spelling of words and to word process or use a lettering kit to make your exhibit appear polished.

Next, put together the incomplete circuit shown in Fig. 2-2. The source of the electric current is the two D-cell batteries (2 D-cells wired in series—one after the other as shown). Connect one of the long wires to one pole of the batteries. Connect one end of the short wire to the other pole of the battery and the other end of the short wire to the light bulb socket.

Figure 2-2

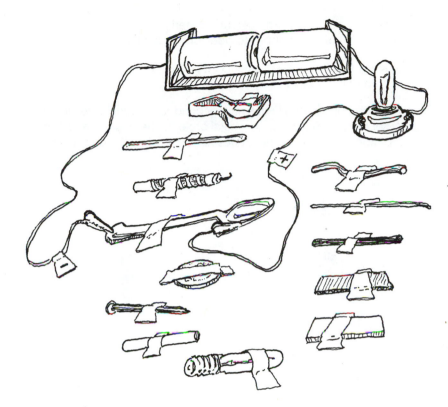

Connect the other long wire to the other side of the light bulb socket. The alligator clips at the ends of the two long wires will be used to touch opposite ends of the objects being tested.

Label a "+" on a small label, and wrap it around the end of the wire that leads to the positive pole of the batteries. Label a "−" on another small label and wrap it around the end of the wire connected to the negative pole of the batteries.

The instructions at this exhibit might read as follows:

To find out which of the test items conduct electricity, touch one end of the object with the alligator clip marked "+." *Briefly* touch the opposite end of the object being tested with the alligator clip marked "−." If the bulb lights, what does it tell you about the object's ability to conduct electricity? What do you know if the bulb doesn't light? (Answers: If the bulb lights, the object is a conductor. If it doesn't light, the object is not a conductor.)

Test each of the items. Which items are electrical conductors? Which items appear to be nonconductors? (Answers: Answers will vary depending on the materials tested, but generally, metallic items are conductors, nonmetallic materials are nonconductors.)

A flashlight bulb is provided so that you can find out where electric current enters and leaves the bulb in order to make it light. Do you think the metal base of the bulb is a conductor?

Test the small metal bead at the bottom of the bulb. Is it a conductor? How about the ceramic material around the metal bead? Is it a conductor? On what two places do you have to touch the bulb with wires to make it light? (Answers:

The metal base is a conductor. The ceramic material is not a conductor. To make the bulb light, touch the opposite sides of the metal bead with both wires.)

How do you know that the bulb's filament is a conductor? (Answer: It glows when connected to the battery.)

Which parts of the outside of a D-cell battery conduct current? Does it depend on the brand of D-cell? (Answers: The metal areas at the positive and negative ends of the battery are conductors. It does not depend on the brand of the battery.)

A hands-on battery

A battery contains several electric cells. Sometimes we refer to a single electric cell as a battery. For example, a D-cell is often called a *flashlight battery*. In any case, an *electric cell* usually has two different metals that constitute the poles, terminals, or electrodes of the cell. The electrodes are in contact with an electrolyte that lies between them. The *electrolyte* is a conductor of electric charge and serves as a source of charge for the electrodes.

In a D-cell, the electrolyte consists of a moist mixture of powdered carbon, manganese dioxide, and ammonium chloride. The positive electrode of the cell is a carbon rod, which is immersed in the electrolyte. The zinc case, the negative pole of the cell, encloses and surrounds the cell's electrolyte.

In a lead storage battery, lead and lead dioxide-coated lead are the electrodes of the cells that make up the battery, and sulfuric acid is the electrolyte. The electrical systems of automobiles and golf carts are powered by lead storage batteries.

At one of the electrodes (the negative one) in an electric cell, electrons are ready to be released. At the other electrode (the positive one), electrons, if available, are taken up. One metal serves as the electron "releaser," the other as the electron "absorber." If the electrodes are connected by a wire, electrons flow from the negative to the positive electrode. The energy available in these electrons can be used to produce light, turn motors, or make toast.

In this exhibit, the electrodes consist of two different metals; the electrolyte is the human body. Because our body fluids contain salt, we are conductors of electric charge. This is particularly true of the perspiration that makes our skin moist or even sweaty. By connecting the two metal electrodes to a sensitive meter that measures the flow of electric charge, the small current that flows through a human body can be detected. The current is small because the body resists the flow of current, and as your patrons can discover for themselves, two bodies together offer more resistance to the flow of charge than one body alone.

In this exhibit, zinc or aluminum is used as one electrode and copper as the other. Both zinc and aluminum have a greater tendency to release electrons than copper, therefore, the copper is the positive electrode and either zinc or aluminum is the negative electrode.

Materials

➢ sheet of copper, appx. 4 inches on a side
➢ sheet of zinc or aluminum, appx. 4 inches on a side
➢ board, appx. 1 foot square
➢ transparent tape
➢ wire strippers
➢ 2, 1-foot-long PVC-insulated wires
➢ 2 alligator clips
➢ microammeter
➢ self-adhesive labels
➢ table

Tape the edges of the sheet of copper and the sheet of zinc (or aluminum) to opposite ends of the board as shown in Fig. 2-3. Rest the board on a table. Leave at least part of the metal edges untaped so wires can be connected to them.

Figure 2-3

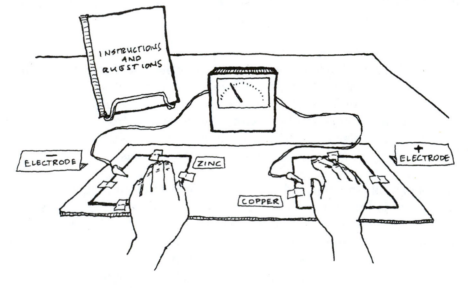

Use the wire strippers to remove approximately 1 inch of insulation from the ends of the two wires. Affix the alligator clips to one end of each of the two wires. Attach the alligator clip of one wire to the copper sheet and connect the other end of the wire to the positive lead of the microammeter. Attach the alligator clip of the second wire to the zinc or aluminum sheet and connect the other wire end to the negative lead of the same meter.

Usually one or both of the meter leads are marked with "+" and "−" signs. Identify the metal plates and the microammeter with self-adhesive labels.

The instructions to your museum patrons, which can be quite simple, might read as follows:

Place one of your hands on the copper sheet and the other hand on the zinc (or aluminum) sheet. Look at the needle of the microammeter to see if your body and the two metals behave like a battery and produce an electric current. What do you observe? (Answer: The needle on the meter indicates a current.)

If your hands are dry, wash them and then return to this exhibit while they are still damp. Is the current more or less than it was when you touched the metals with dry hands? (Answer: The current is greater with damp hands.)

What happens if you touch the copper plate with both hands? What happens if you touch the zinc (or aluminum) plate with both hands? (Answer: There is no current.)

Is there an electric current if you join hands with a partner and you touch one metal while your partner touches the other? (Answer: Yes, there is a current, but less than with one person.)

Of course, you can add more information about batteries and electricity to this exhibit if you wish. However, the main attraction is the human hands-on battery.

Electricity from fruits and vegetables

Just as your body can serve as an electrolyte, so too can fruits and vegetables. This exhibit might be an ongoing one in which museum visitors can test the electric current from a different fruit or vegetable each day. You might begin with a lemon followed by an apple, an orange, a banana, a pear, a peach, a potato, and so on. You will find that one of the best electrolytes is a pimento-stuffed olive.

Materials

- variety of fruits and vegetables
- paper plates
- 1 copper and 1 aluminum nail or heavy strips of copper and aluminum (or zinc), appx. 2 inches × ½ inch
- heavy-duty scissors
- 2 PVC-insulated wires, appx. 1 foot long, with alligator clips attached to one end
- microammeter (meter reads millionths of an ampere)
- steel wool
- scissors

The copper and aluminum nails or the heavy strips of copper and aluminum or copper and zinc will be the electrodes. If you will be using strips of aluminum or zinc and copper, cut the strips so that they form points at one end.

Attach the ends of each wire to the leads of the microammeter as shown in Fig. 2-4. If you use a zero-center meter, it doesn't matter which meter lead is connected to which electrode. If the meter needle moves only clockwise, the copper electrode should be connected to the positive lead of the meter, and the aluminum or zinc electrode should be connected to the negative lead. The electrodes should be rinsed in water and cleaned with steel wool each day.

Figure 2-4

The instructions to your museum patrons might read as follows:

Stick the copper and aluminum nails (or metal strips) that are attached to the microammeter into the fruit or vegetable found on the paper plate. Watch the needle of the meter. Do the fruit and the two metals behave like a battery and produce an electric current? How much current in microamperes (millionths of an ampere) is produced? (Answers: Yes, a current is produced. The size of the current varies.)

Come back tomorrow and try a different fruit or vegetable. Which fruit or vegetable do you think provides the largest current? (Answers will vary.)

An electric generator

Prior to 1831, electricity had been produced only by means of batteries, but after learning about Hans Christian Oersted's discovery that electric currents produce magnetic fields, Michael Faraday reasoned that it should be possible to obtain electricity from magnets. Faraday set out to prove that he was right. He placed coils of wire near strong magnets, but no currents could be detected in the wires. Finally, in 1831, he discovered the secret to making electricity from magnets. In this exhibit, those who visit your museum can make the same discovery.

Materials

➢ 24-foot-long, enamel-coated copper wire
➢ D-cell battery
➢ tape
➢ sandpaper
➢ board, appx. 4 inches square
➢ 2 PVC-insulated copper wires, each with an alligator clip on one end
➢ zero-center microammeter
➢ bar magnet

Wind the 24-foot-long wire around the D-cell. Carefully slip the wire from the battery to retain the wire's shape. Use a small piece of tape to temporarily hold the coils in place (Fig. 2-5). Remove approximately 1 inch of the insulation from both ends of the coiled wire with the sandpaper. Tape the coil in an upright position on the small board.

Connect both of the sanded ends of the coiled wire to a zero-center microammeter with the alligator clips (Fig. 2-5). Place the board on a tabletop with the bar magnet.

The information and instructions accompanying this exhibit might read as follows:

To see what Faraday discovered, watch the meter as you move the bar magnet in and out of the coil of wire. Have you produced an electric current? How do you know? Does the speed with which you move the magnet in and out of the coil affect the size of the current? Does the direction of current (given by the movement of the meter's needle left or right of center) depend on which direction you move the magnet? Does the initial direction of the current depend on the pole (north or south) of the magnet that first enters the coil? (Answers: Yes, there is a current. The meter indicates that charge is flowing. The faster the magnet moves, the greater the current. The direction of the current changes with the direction of motion of the magnet. The initial direction of the current depends on which pole first enters the coil.)

Have a friend hold the magnet still while you move the board to which the coil is taped toward and then away from the magnet. Is a current produced? Does it matter whether it's the coil or the magnet that moves? (Answers: Yes, a current is produced. The current is produced regardless of whether it's the coil or the magnet that moves.)

Figure 2-5

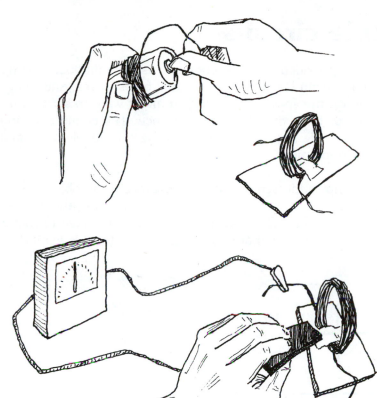

Simple circuits

The exhibits provided in this section consist of a number of simple circuits made from D-cell batteries, small bulbs, wires, and switches. Depending on the space available, you might want to set up the circuits two or three at a time or all at once. The circuit combinations form a reasonable sequence of exhibits. Be sure to use bulbs and D-cells that are identical.

Figure 2-6 shows the symbols used to represent the objects—batteries (and holders), bulbs (and sockets), switches, and wires—that make up the circuits. These symbols eliminate the need for detailed drawings of the circuits that you are preparing for this exhibit.

Figure 2-6

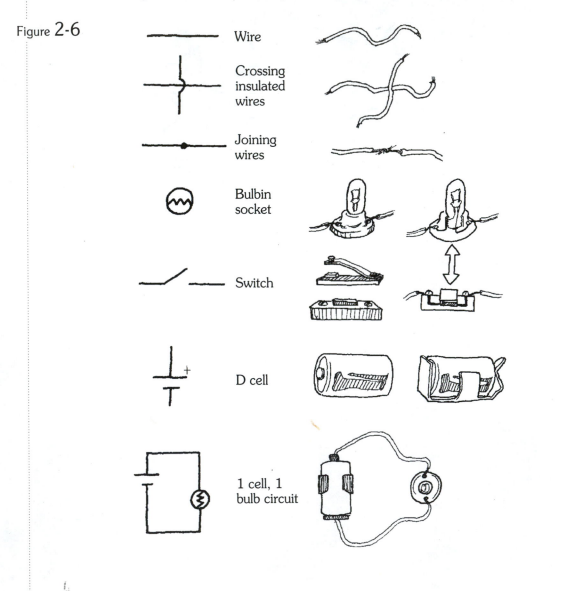

Wire

Crossing insulated wires

Joining wires

Bulb in socket

Switch

D cell

1 cell, 1 bulb circuit

Since the wires in these circuits do not have to be connected by your visitors, you do not need to use wires with alligator clips. Insulation can be removed from the ends of the wires by using wire strippers. The wires can then be connected to bulb sockets, switches, and battery holders with screws or clips. If possible, choose bulbs that light when connected to a single battery. If you use threaded sockets, you must use threaded flashlight bulbs.

Because of internal changes within the cells, batteries connected to circuits that carry larger currents discharge more rapidly than circuits that carry smaller currents. For example, a circuit with two bulbs in series carries significantly less current than a single bulb circuit or two bulbs wired in parallel. Consequently, you should be prepared to replace batteries when bulbs glow noticeably dimmer.

One- and two-bulb circuits
Materials

➢ 3 threaded flashlight bulbs
➢ 3 threaded sockets for flashlight bulbs
➢ 2 D-cells
➢ 2 push-button switches
➢ 6-inch lengths of PVC-insulated copper wire
➢ wire strippers
➢ 2 battery holders
➢ transparent tape
➢ self-adhesive labels
➢ tabletop

Figure 2-7a shows two simple circuits that should be exhibited together. Both circuits are easy to put together on a tabletop. Before building the circuits, use wire strippers to remove about ½ inch of insulation from the ends of each wire.

Figure 2-7a

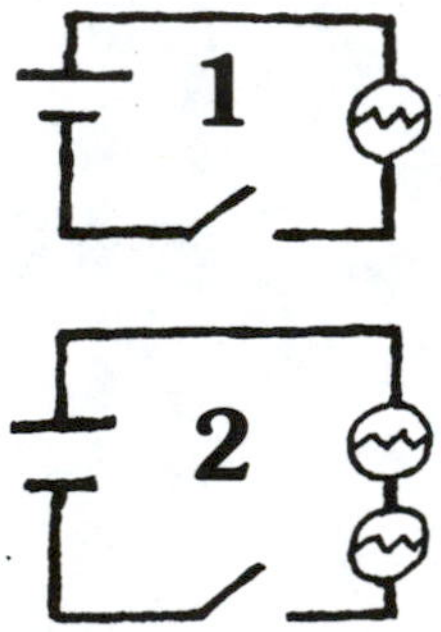

To make the upper circuit in Fig. 2-7a, wire one flashlight bulb to one D-cell battery through a switch. To connect the two ends of the battery to the flashlight bulb through wires, press the switch. Because wires are good conductors of electricity, the bulb lights. Label the switch "Circuit 1."

Make the lower circuit in Fig. 2-7a by wiring two bulbs in series (one after the other) and connecting the wire to one battery. Label the switch "Circuit 2" so viewers can respond quickly to instructions.

The information and question that might accompany this exhibit is as follows:

DO NOT ATTEMPT TO CHANGE ANY OF THE CIRCUITS OR THE EXHIBIT MIGHT NOT WORK AS IT SHOULD. To view this exhibit, press the switch (push button) that allows charge to flow through the circuit with one bulb, Circuit 1. Then press the switch that allows a charge to flow through the circuit with two bulbs wired in series (one bulb after the other), Circuit 2. Which circuit has the brighter bulb(s)? Can you explain why? (Answer: The bulb in Circuit 1 is brighter. With two bulbs, the length of the thin filament through which charge flows is doubled. Thus, the resistance to the flow of electric charge is doubled. Consequently, less charge flows through two bulbs than through one.)

Bulbs in series and parallel circuits
Materials

➤ 5 threaded flashlight bulbs
➤ 5 threaded sockets for bulbs
➤ 3 D-cells
➤ 3 battery holders
➤ 3 push-button switches
➤ 12, 6-inch-long PVC-insulated copper wires
➤ wire strippers
➤ self-adhesive labels
➤ tabletop
➤ ruler

Figure 2-7b shows three simple circuits. Before building the circuits, measure and cut the 12 wires and then use the wire strippers to remove about ½ inch of insulation from the ends of each wire.

Figure 2-7b

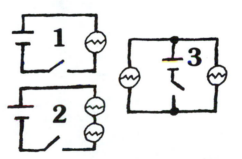

One circuit consists of one flashlight bulb connected to one battery through a switch. To connect the two ends of the battery to the bulb through wires, press the button on the switch. Because the wires are good conductors of electricity, the bulb lights. This bulb serves as a means of comparing bulb brightness in the other two circuits. Label this circuit "Circuit 1."

The next circuit has two bulbs wired in series (one after the other) and connected to one battery. Label this one "Circuit 2." The last circuit has two bulbs wired in parallel; that is, the circuit divides so that charge can follow either of the two paths that lead through the bulb and back to the battery. Label this "Circuit 3."

The information and questions that might accompany this exhibit are as follows:

DO NOT ATTEMPT TO CHANGE ANY OF THE CIRCUITS OR EXHIBIT MIGHT NOT WORK AS IT SHOULD. To view this exhibit, press the switch (push button) that allows a charge to flow through the circuit with one bulb, which is labeled

"Circuit 1." This bulb serves as the brightness standard for the bulbs in the other two circuits.

Next, press the switch that allows charge to flow through Circuit 2, which has two bulbs wired in series (one bulb after the other). Which circuit, 1 or 2, has the brighter bulb(s)? Can you explain why? (Answers: The bulb in Circuit 1 is brighter than the bulbs in Circuit 2 because the resistance to the flow of electric charge is doubled in Circuit 2. Consequently, less charge flows through two bulbs than one.)

Finally, press the switch that allows charge to flow through Circuit 3, which has two bulbs wired in parallel (side by side) so that charge can follow either of the two paths that lead through a bulb and back to the battery. Which circuit, 1 or 3, has the brighter bulb(s)? In which circuit, 2 or 3, are the bulbs brighter? Can you explain why? (Answers: The bulbs in Circuits 1 and 3 appear to have about the same brightness. The explanation is more complicated than for bulbs in series, and the brightness isn't exactly the same, but in both circuits single bulbs are connected to a single battery.)

Batteries in series and in parallel
Materials

➤ 3 threaded flashlight bulbs
➤ 3 threaded sockets for bulbs
➤ 5 D-cells
➤ 3 push-button switches
➤ 5 battery holders
➤ 3, 6-inch-long PVC-insulated wires
➤ wire strippers
➤ self-adhesive labels
➤ tabletop
➤ ruler

Figure 2-7c shows three simple circuits. Before building the circuits, measure and cut the 3 wires and then use the wire strippers to remove about ½ inch of insulation from the ends of each wire.

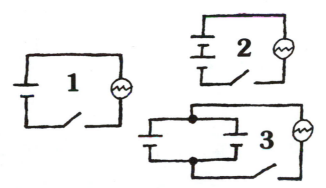

Figure 2-7c

The first circuit is made using one flashlight bulb connected to one D-cell battery through a switch. Pressing the button on the switch connects the two ends of the battery to the bulb through wires. Because the wires are good conductors of electricity, the bulb lights. This bulb serves as a means of comparing bulb brightness in the other two circuits. Put this circuit together and label it "Circuit 1."

For the next circuit, wire two batteries in series (one after the other) and connect them to one bulb. Label this "Circuit 2." For the last circuit, wire the two batteries in parallel; that is, the circuit divides so the charge can follow either of the two paths that lead through the battery and back to the single bulb. Label this "Circuit 3."

The information and questions that might accompany this exhibit are as follows:

DO NOT ATTEMPT TO CHANGE ANY OF THE CIRCUITS. To view this exhibit, press the switch (push button) that allows charge to flow through the circuit with one bulb and one battery, which is labeled "Circuit 1." This bulb serves as a brightness standard for the bulbs in the other two circuits.

Next, press the switch that allows charge to flow through Circuit 2, which has two batteries connected in series (one after the other). In which circuit, 1 or 2, is the bulb brighter? Can you explain why? (Answers: The bulb in Circuit 2 is brighter than the bulb in Circuit 1 because it is connected to two batteries. Each battery provides some energy to the charges. Passing through two batteries provides nearly twice as much energy per charge. This energy is released in the bulb as heat and light.)

Finally, press the switch that allows charge to flow through Circuit 3, which has two batteries wired in parallel (side by side) so that charge can follow either of the two paths that lead through a battery and back to the single bulb. In which circuit, 1 or 3, is the bulb brighter? Can you explain why? (Answers: The bulbs in Circuits 1 and 3 appear to have about the same brightness. In each case, charge passes through a single battery where it receives its energy. In fact, two batteries in parallel can be thought of as a single D-cell that has been made twice as big.)

An electric quiz board

You can use your knowledge of electricity to make a quiz board like the one shown in Fig. 2-8. The quiz board can be used in any exhibit in which you ask people to match questions with answers. For example, you could ask people to match photographs of animals with drawings, casts, or photographs of the animals' footprints. (See the section "Animal tracks" in Part 6.) Your quiz board can be used for social studies, English, math, and foreign language exhibits as well as for science.

Figure 2-8

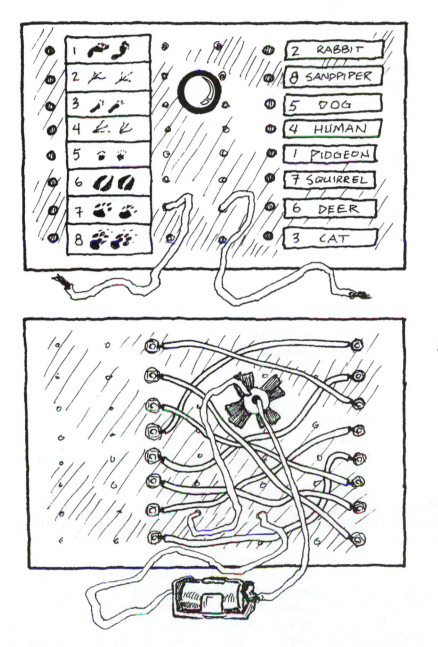

Materials

> - pegboard, appx. 11 × 14 inches
> - wide-headed, short bolts (1 bolt for each question and 1 bolt for each answer presented on the pegboard)
> - washers and nuts (2 washers and 1 nut for each bolt used)
> - self-adhesive labels
> - 3 PVC-insulated copper wires, appx. 24 inches long
> - 10 or more short PVC-insulated copper wires, appx. 6 to 10 inches long (one for each item on the pegboard)
> - wire strippers
> - drill
> - flashlight bulb
> - socket for bulb
> - transparent packing tape
> - battery holder
> - D-cell battery
> - screwdriver and pliers (screwdriver type depends on bolt type)
> - tabletop

The bolts you select must fit the holes in the pegboard. Arrange the bolts in a vertical row as shown in Fig. 2-8. Affix the labels next to the row of bolts on the left. The labels should have a number and a question, the name of an item, or as shown, a drawing. Remember to word process or use a lettering kit for your labels and to double check your spelling.

Next to the bolts on the right side of the board, affix the labels with the answers to the questions. The answers should not be located directly next to the question they answer.

On the back of the pegboard (Fig. 2-8), add two washers and a nut to each bolt. Strip approximately 1 inch of insulation from both ends of each of the shorter wires. To connect each question on the left side of the board to the correct answer on the right, put the bare ends of each of the wires between the washers on each bolt and tighten the nuts securely.

Have an adult make a hole in the center of the pegboard with a drill. Use a bit large enough for the flashlight bulb to be inserted through the board. Tape the bulb's socket securely to the back of the board.

Next, strip approximately 1 inch of insulation from one of the long wires. Connect the bare end of this wire to one terminal of the battery holder that contains the battery behind the board. Run the other end of this wire through a hole at the bottom of the pegboard to the front of the board. Strip approximately 1 inch of insulation from one of the other long wires and connect one end of this wire to the other side of the battery. Connect the other end of the wire to one side of the light bulb socket.

Strip approximately 1 inch of insulation from the last long wire, and connect one end of this wire to the other side of the light bulb socket. Run this long wire through a hole at the bottom of the pegboard to the front of the board (Fig. 2-8).

Instructions to exhibit visitors might be something like the following:

Hold the bare end of the wire on the left against the head of the bolt beside a question or item. Touch the bare end of the wire on the right to the head of the bolt beside what you think is the correct answer to the question or item. If the bulb lights, you are correct.

Pinhole images

At one time, the *camera obscura* was popular among artists. It was simply a lightproof room with a very tiny hole on one wall. When light from an object outside the room came through the pinhole, an image of the object was seen on a wall or canvas opposite the hole. The image made it possible for artists to paint accurate copies of the real world.

In this exhibit, viewers have an opportunity to see pinhole images and to discover that the images are really inverted and turned left for right.

Materials

- heavy cardboard box, appx. 8 inches on a side
- heavy-duty scissors
- clear bulb with a vertical or horizontal straight filament, 60 or 75 watts
- portable bulb socket for a horizontal filament bulb or a socket to fit a vertical filament bulb
- transparent tape
- 2, 8½ × 11 sheets of black construction paper
- 2, 8½ × 11 sheets of white paper
- 2 sheets of stiff cardboard, appx. 11 × 26 inches
- pencil
- copy of Fig. 2-10
- dark or dimly lit location

Ask an adult to help you make the cuts in the light box shown in Fig. 2-9. Cut off the box-top flaps, then cut some holes in the bottom of the box so that heat can escape. If the bulb you will be using contains a vertical filament, put it into the socket and place it under the center of the inverted box. *Be sure the bulb does not touch the box; this would be a fire hazard.*

If you are using a bulb that contains a horizontal filament, make a hole in one side of the box for the portable socket to fit in to. Put the socket into the hole and add the bulb. Be sure to turn the bulb so that its filament rests vertically (*see* Fig. 2-9).

Invert the box and cut two openings approximately 2 inches square on opposite sides of the box. Align the holes with the bulb's filament. Cut two masks made from black construction paper and tape them over the openings.

Figure 2-9

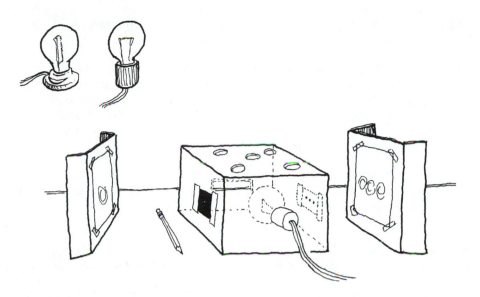

On one side of the box, make a single pinhole at the center of the black paper covering the hole. On the opposite side of the box, make three pinholes close together on the mask.

On a side perpendicular to the sides with the pinholes, cut a hole large enough for a viewer to insert his or her hand while holding a pencil.

Bend the cardboard sheets as shown in Fig. 2-9, and tape the white paper to the cardboard to make two screens. Stand the sheets upright, and place one screen near the single pinhole and the other on the opposite side of the box near the three pinholes.

If your exhibit location is not dimly lit, you need to reduce the lighting so that viewers can see the images on the white screens.

Display the diagram shown in Fig. 2-10 near your box along with the pencil.

Figure 2-10

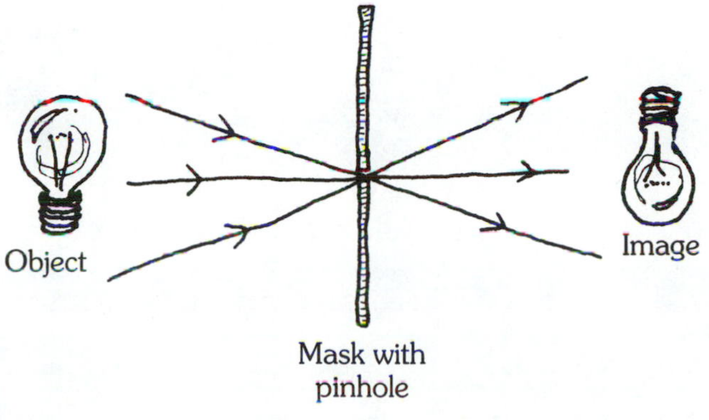

Object   Image

Mask with
pinhole

Instructions and questions appropriate for this exhibit can be placed near the box. They might read as follows:

This box contains a bulb with a brightly lit filament. On one side of the box is one tiny pinhole through which light can escape. If you look closely, you can see an image of the filament on the white screen near the pinhole. What happens to the size of the image as you move the screen farther from the box? What happens when you move it closer to the box? (Answers: The image grows larger. The image becomes smaller.)

Is the image inverted? To find out, slowly move the tip of the pencil provided up and down between the bulb and the pinhole so that its shadow can be seen on the screen. A hole has been cut in the box so you can do this. What do you discover? (Answer: The image is inverted.)

How can you find out if the image is also turned right for left? To find out, move the pencil horizontally in front of the filament. (Answer: The image is reversed.)

Can you explain how the image you see is formed? (Answer: See the diagram to best explain the formation of the image.)

This box has three pinholes on the opposite side. How many images of the filament are there on the screen near these pinholes? (Answers: Three pinholes produce three images.)

Color a soap film

If you have ever blown soap bubbles, you know that beautiful colors form in the soap film. The colors form because of the reflection and interference (overlapping) of light of different wave lengths. To enable visitors to see these colors more clearly, you can build a device that allows them to make a large, flat soap film and then watch it drain.

Materials

> 2 drinking straws
> 3-foot-long piece of twine
> 2, 2-foot-long pieces of twine
> soap solution
> 2, 1-x-2-inch boards, 2 feet long
> 1, 1-x-2-inch board, 1 foot long
> 1, 1-x-4-inch board, 1 foot long
> small nails and hammer or wood glue and clamps
> drill with small bit
> washer
> shallow pan longer than drinking straws and that can fit inside the finished frame you must build
> cup hook or other small hook
> ruler
> scissors
> optional: several sheets of dark construction paper, tape, and pegboard

If you don't have prepared soap solution, make your own soap solution by adding ⅔ cup of dish liquid and 1 tablespoon (approximately 30 drops) of glycerine to 1 gallon of soft water. The soap solution works best if it ages several days.

The frame on which the soap film forms is made with the two drinking straws and the 3-foot-long piece of twine. Measure and cut the twine to the correct length. Run the twine through the straws to form a rectangle (Fig. 2-11a), tie the ends together, and move the knot inside the lower straw in the frame.

Figure 2-11a

Run one of the 2-foot-long pieces of twine through one of the straws that make up the frame. Tie the ends together. You will use this shorter string to lower the frame into the soapy liquid.

Use the lumber to build the simple frame shown in Fig. 2-11b. Ask an adult to drill a small hole through the center of the upper horizontal piece. Run the second 2-foot-long piece of twine through the hole to the other string that is connected to the upper straw. Tie a washer to the end of the string (Fig. 2-11b) to serve as a handle and to prevent it from slipping back through the hole into the soapy liquid.

Figure 2-11b

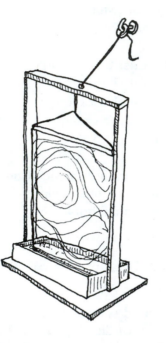

Insert the cup hook or the other hook in a spot above and behind the frame where the washer can rest on it. The film needs to remain in place so patrons can look at it from various angles. Perhaps you can set the exhibit up on a tabletop against a wall with pegboard behind it.

Pour the soap solution into the long shallow pan that fits within the frame. Lower the straw and string frame into the liquid. Be sure both straws and the entire string are submerged. Pull up on the washer. Watch a soap film form between the two straws as the top straw is pulled upward. Fasten the washer to the hook, then enjoy the color show as you watch the soap film drain.

The colors are brightest if a dark background is placed behind the soap film. You could tape several pieces of dark construction paper to some cardboard that you bend and stand upright behind the soap film or tape the dark paper to a pegboard or a wall behind the soap film.

The light, preferably natural light that reflects off the film, should come from behind the viewers. As they watch the film drain, they can see wide bands of color.

In addition to instructions on creating the soap film, you might include questions like the following on your exhibit card:

What happens to the widths of the bands of color as the soap film drains? How many different colors can you see? (Answers: The bands grow closer together. Many colors are seen.)

After the film has drained for a time, you will see a dark region at the top of the film. The film in this dark area is very thin. If you think that no film is there, touch the dark region with your finger. What happens? (Answer: The film breaks.)

Can you see images reflected from the film? How do they differ from the images you see in a mirror? (Answers: Yes, images are visible, but the colors of the image are not the same as the colors of the reflected object.)

Your fingerprints

No two people have the same fingerprints, which is why fingerprints are one of the major clues detectives look for at the scene of a crime. Visitors to this exhibit record their fingerprints, classify them, and leave the records as part of an ongoing exhibit. If possible, set up the exhibit near a sink or lavatory so people can wash their hands immediately after they leave the exhibit.

Materials
➤ black ink foam stamp pad
➤ white 8½ × 11 paper
➤ pencil or pen
➤ display of fingerprint patterns
➤ shoebox
➤ bulletin board or corkboard
➤ tabletop
➤ access to a photocopier
➤ access to a word processor
➤ scissors
➤ thumbtacks

Word process or print a form like the one shown in Fig. 2-12. Create it so that there are two forms to one 8½ × 11 page. If you are using a word processor, you should be able to just copy it once you've created it.

Print out the forms, and make approximately 20 photocopies. Cut the photocopies in half and place them on a tabletop near the stamp pad so visitors can make ink impressions of their fingerprints on the forms.

Push the table against a wall and position the bulletin board or the corkboard behind the exhibit. Tack up the diagram of fingerprints shown in Fig. 2-12. Put the shoebox next to the sheets of paper.

Ask visitors to make their prints on the paper you have provided. After a person records his or her prints, place the record in a shoebox until there are enough to display.

When you gather enough prints, post them as part of the exhibit so that visitors can compare their fingerprints with those of other people. They might also compare the patterns of their prints with those patterns on your fingerprint diagram.

Figure 2-12

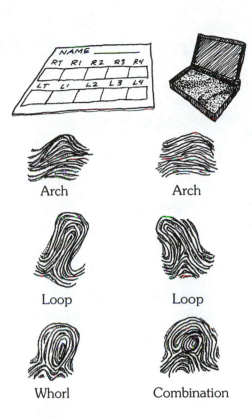

Arch   Arch

Loop   Loop

Whorl   Combination

The instructions for recording fingerprints might be similar to the following:

Record your fingerprints on one of the forms provided. First, write your name in the space provided. Open the ink pad and press your right thumb against the black surface. Carefully press your inked thumb onto the paper in the proper space (the one labeled RT). Be careful not to smudge the print. Repeat the procedure for each finger of your right hand (R1, R2, R3, and R4), then record the prints from your left hand.

Questions accompanying your display of fingerprint records might be similar to the following:

Compare the patterns in your prints with those in the drawing. How many of your prints contain an arch pattern, a loop pattern, a whorl pattern, or a pattern that is a combination of the others? Do all your fingerprints have the same pattern (arch, loop, whorl) or do they vary from finger to finger? (Answers will vary.)

Is any one pattern more common than another? Do people tend to have the same pattern (loop, arch, whorl) on all their fingers, or do patterns vary from finger to finger? (Answers will vary.)

Please leave the sheet with your fingerprint patterns in the shoebox provided; they will become part of an ongoing collection of prints.

What does a million look like?

We all use numbers as large as a million to describe the populations of cities or the price of a lovely house, but can you visualize a million of anything? You might ask this question as an introduction to this math-related exhibit.

Materials

➤ typewriter or word processor
➤ 8½ × 11 sheets of white paper
➤ 1 or 2 large spring-type binders
➤ access to a photocopier

Using a typewriter or word processor, make rows of x's like the one below on a sheet of the white paper. Make 2,500 such letters on a single page (50 rows of 50 x's equal 2,500).

xxxxxxxxxxxxxxxxxxxxxxxxxxxxxxxxxxxxxxxxxxxxxxxxxxx

Make 399 copies of this page to get 1 million x's. Place the 400 pages (or 200 if you use both sides of the paper) in the binders so people can flip through them.

An introduction taped to the front of the binder might read as follows:

If you have never seen a million of anything, here is your chance to do so. One million x's are inside this binder. If you flip through the pages, you can say that you have seen a million things in one place.

Imagine a book made of $100 bills. If each page holds 10 bills, how many pages would the book contain to be worth $1 million? (Answer: The book will have 1,000 pages.)

An alternative approach to this exhibit is to use a long hallway to display the 400 pages containing your 2,500 x's. This display requires using 260 square feet of wall space and might be worth doing as a week-long exhibit. Add a few pages each day until all 1 million x's are on the wall.

Estimating

In this math-related exhibit, visitors can test their skills at estimating the number of dots on a page.

Materials

➢ typewriter or word processor
➢ 8½ × 11 sheets of white paper
➢ metric ruler

Using a typewriter or a word processor, make a row of dots (periods) without any spaces between them. Then make as many single-spaced lines of dots as will fit onto the page. If you are using a word processor, simply copy and paste the first line of dots over and over until the page is filled.

The instructions accompanying your page of dots might read as follows:

You can see lots of dots on the paper displayed here. You might go crazy trying to count all of them, but to find the number of dots, you can make a very good estimate by using a ruler and common sense.

With the metric ruler provided, count the number of dots per centimeter. Then measure the length of a line and count the number of lines. With this information, you should be able to make a good estimate of the total number of dots on the page. What is your estimate of the number of dots on the page? (Answers depend on the sheet you prepare, but you can estimate by counting the dots in one line and multiplying by the number of lines.)

Other ideas for exhibits

➤ Display photographs that contain a large number of objects, such as an aerial photo of a crowd at an athletic event. Then ask viewers to estimate the number of birds, people, or other objects in the photographs.

➤ Ask people to design an experiment to estimate the number of stars visible in the sky, the number of blades of grass on an athletic field, the number of grains of rice in a box of rice, the number of words in this book, the number of hairs on their heads, and so on. Give prizes for the best responses.

➤ Build a small weather station with instruments that can be read by exhibit visitors. You might include displays showing temperature, wind speed, wind direction, humidity, air pressure, and rainfall. Ask visitors to submit their weather predictions for tomorrow based on the data in the exhibit.

➤ Make a photographic display of water clocks to accompany your own water clock that measures time in hours.

➤ Develop an exhibit to show how the world looks through various colored filters, including rose-colored glasses.

➤ Exhibit an electromagnet that lifts a nail when you close a switch and drops the nail when you open the switch.

➤ Build electric circuits that include voltmeters and ammeters. Show how voltages and currents are affected by the number of batteries, the number of bulbs, and whether the bulbs and batteries are in series or parallel.

➤ Show how electricity and magnetism are combined to make an electric motor.

➤ Invite people to make giant soap bubbles using the soap film frame made from drinking straws and string.

Part 3

Interactive exhibits

This section contains more hands-on exhibits but with an added dimension. The exhibits require your museum visitors to perform actions within an experiment. The actions performed lead visitors to the answer, to a question, or to the discovery of a pattern or law of nature.

The law of reflection

This exhibit teaches visitors about the law of reflection. Your patrons will discover on their own how this law works with the use of a narrow light beam and a mirror mounted on the baseline of a large protractor.

Materials

➤ cardboard box, appx. 1 foot on a side
➤ heavy-duty scissors
➤ 8½ × 11 sheet of black construction paper
➤ transparent tape
➤ clear light bulb with a straight vertical filament
➤ socket to fit bulb
➤ plane mirror, appx. 2 × 3 inches
➤ 8½ × 11 sheet of white paper
➤ 8-inch-square piece of plywood (or other thin board)
➤ large protractor
➤ ruler
➤ black ink pen
➤ sharp knife
➤ rubber band
➤ wooden block, appx. 3 × 3 × 1 inches
➤ wood glue

To produce a narrow beam of light, make a small light box like the one described in "Pinhole images" in Part 2.

Begin by asking an adult to help you cut off the flaps at the top of the box. Then cut some holes in the bottom of the box so that heat can escape. Invert the box, and cut a 4-x-4-inch opening centered at the base on one side.

Cut a mask from the black construction paper that is slightly larger than the opening in the box. Cut a narrow slit about ¹⁄₁₆ × 4 inches long in the paper. Tape the paper over the opening in the box so that the slit is vertical.

Put the bulb in the socket and place it under the center of the box. Be sure the bulb does not touch the box (Fig. 3-1); this would be a fire hazard.

The light beam emerging from the box must be narrow and well defined. If it is not, slightly adjust the bulb or box. If the beam is still not narrow enough, you need to make a second mask with a narrower slit. Fold the sides of the second mask and stand it in front of the first mask so that the light has to pass through both slits (Fig. 3-2).

Figure 3-1

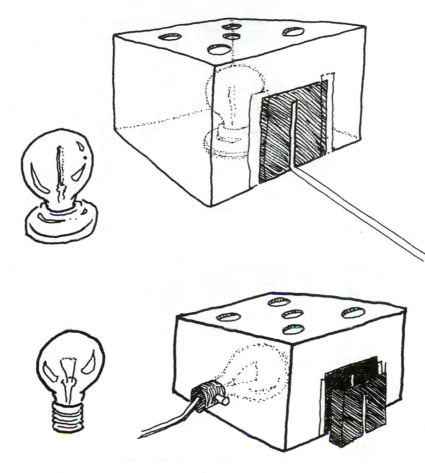
Figure 3-2

Next, build the device to support the mirror. Tape the sheet of white paper to the plywood or other thin board. Place the protractor near the center of the paper and mark angles at 10-degree intervals on both sides of the protractor's 90-degree line. Use black ink and a ruler to draw and label the angle lines as shown in Fig. 3-3a. With an adult's help, carefully cut the paper along the baseline with the sharp knife.

Place the mirror against the wooden block and use the rubber band to hold it in place (Fig. 3-3b). The mirror's reflective side should face away from the block's surface. Place the block and mirror on the board so that the front of the mirror lies along the baseline as shown in Fig. 3-3c. Use the wood glue to fasten the block to the board.

When the glue is dry, place the board and mirror in front of the light box. Direct the narrow light beam so that it passes along an angle line on the paper to the point on the baseline where all the angle lines meet. At that point, the beam is reflected off the mirror's surface along another angle line.

Figure 3-3

A

B

C

Exhibit instructions might read as follows:

The degrees of the angles on the paper are measured from the center (0°) line, which is perpendicular to the mirror. Turn the board so that the narrow light beam strikes the mirror along a particular angle. This angle is called the *angle of incidence.*

The reflected beam also makes an angle measured from the same perpendicular line. This second angle is called the *angle of reflection.* How does the angle of incidence compare with the angle of reflection? (Answer: They are equal.)

Measure different angles of incidence. How do the angles of incidence and reflection compare for each angle you try? What can you conclude from this experiment? (Answers: They are the same. The angle of incidence always equals the angle of reflection.)

Double reflection

In this exhibit, viewers learn that the third image seen when two mirrors are at right angles is the result of a double reflection. In other words, what they see is an image of an image. They also discover what happens to the number of images when the angle between the mirrors is decreased.

Materials

- ➤ 6 identical plane mirrors, appx. 2 × 3 inches
- ➤ 3 golf tees
- ➤ 6 blocks of scrap wood or children's blocks
- ➤ 3 sheets of 8½ × 11 white paper
- ➤ masking tape or transparent tape
- ➤ table (optional)
- ➤ chair (optional)
- ➤ protractor
- ➤ ruler
- ➤ pen

Ideally, you should set up this exhibit at eye level. However, a table and chair works adequately, provided visitors can look directly into the mirrors.

Place two mirrors at right angles on a white sheet of paper as shown in Fig. 3-4a. Use the blocks of wood to support the mirrors in an upright position. Tape the wood in place. Draw two black lines 90 degrees apart on the paper to mark the mirrors' positions.

Figure 3-4a

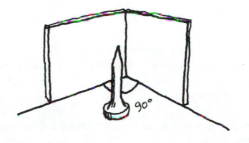

Figure 3-4b

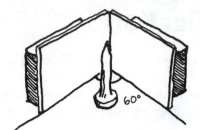

Figure 3-4c

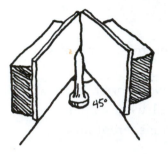

On another sheet of paper, draw two black lines at 60 degrees apart. Place the two mirrors so that they make an angle of 60 degrees (Fig. 3-4b). Repeat on a third sheet of paper but draw the angles at 45 degrees (Fig. 3-4c).

As an added attraction and if your location permits, place two large mirrors on opposite walls so that the mirrors are parallel. Visitors can then answer the last question raised in the exhibit by standing between the mirrors.

Place the golf tees near your printed instructions. Instructions to accompany this exhibit might read as follows:

Begin the experiment with the two mirrors placed at right angles (90 degrees). Make certain the front edges of the mirrors rest on the black lines drawn on the paper.

Stand the upside-down golf tee between the two mirrors. How many images of the golf tee do you see when you look into the two mirrors? How can you explain what you see? (Answers: Three images are seen. The light reflects more than once to produce a third image.)

Now cover the area of one mirror near the line where the two mirrors meet with your hand. What happens? (Answer: The middle image disappears.)

Cover the same region of the other mirror with your hand. What happens now? (Answer: The middle image disappears again.)

You have just shown that the middle image is caused by a double reflection. This middle image is a result of light reflected off both mirrors. The right and left images disappear only when you cover the right and left mirrors respectively.

Turn now to the mirrors that are angled at 60 degrees. How many images do you see? (Answer: Five images are seen when the mirrors are at 60 degrees.)

Finally, look into the mirrors that are angled at 45 degrees. How many images do you see? (Answer: Seven images are seen when the mirrors make a 45-degree angle.)

What happens to the number of images as the angle between the mirrors decreases? How many images would you see if the mirrors were parallel? (Answer: The number of images increases as the angle between the mirrors decreases. If the mirrors are parallel, an infinite number of images can be seen.)

You as others see you

This exhibit shows how a plane mirror forms an image (Fig. 3-5a).
The mirror reflects light rays from an object, which is illustrated as
"O," at angles given by the law of reflection. The rays reflected by
the mirror from each point on the object appear to come from
corresponding points behind the mirror. These points, two of which
are shown, form the image ("I" in Fig. 3-5a). The image is reversed,
like the image you see when you look into a mirror; that is, when
you wink your right eye, your image winks its left eye.

Materials

➤ 2 plane mirrors, at least 6 inches tall
➤ table
➤ masking tape
➤ 2 wooden blocks (large enough to support each mirror in an
upright position)
➤ copy of Fig. 3-5b

Figure 3-5b shows what happens when you place two mirrors at right
angles. Object O forms images I_1 and I_2, however, the third image, I_3,
is formed by a double reflection of the light rays coming from O.
Simply put, the reversed image is reversed again. If you become
object O, your middle image, I_3, winks its right eye when you wink
your right eye.

Figure 3-5a

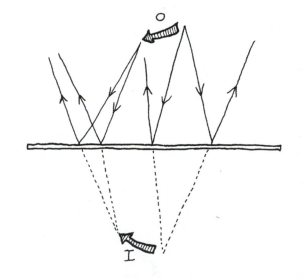

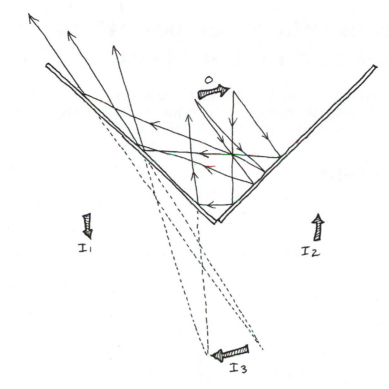

Figure 3-5b

Place the two mirrors at right angles near the edge of the table so a viewer can put his or her face close to the mirrors. The mirrors are at 90 degrees when the middle images fuse to form a single image. Firmly support the mirrors by taping their edges to heavy wooden blocks. Also, provide visitors with a copy of the double reflection shown in Fig. 3-5b.

The instructions and questions placed in front of the mirror might read much like the following:

Put your face close to these two mirrors, which are at right angles. You will see three images of your face. The two images on each side are what you would see if you looked into each mirror separately. Look at one of those two images and wink your right eye. Which eye does your image wink? (Answer: The image winks its left eye.)

Look closely at the middle image. It reveals how others see you. To see why, wink your right eye. Which eye does your middle image wink? (Answer: The middle image winks its right eye.)

Touch your left cheek. Which cheek does your image touch? Can you explain this non-mirrorlike image? (Answers: The image touches its left cheek. The middle image forms from the double reflection of light from your face; it is an image of an image.)

You as others see you when you stand on your head

In this exhibit, visitors see their mirror images reflected as though they were being seen upside-down. This exhibit could be set up beside the previous exhibit or could follow the next one.

Materials

➤ 2 mirrors, at least 6 inches tall
➤ tabletop
➤ masking tape
➤ wooden block (large enough to support one mirror in an upright position)
➤ copy of Fig. 3-5b

Place the two mirrors so that one is horizontal and the other is vertical as shown in Fig. 3-6. Use the masking tape and the wooden block to support the vertical mirror. Provide your visitors with a copy of the double reflection shown in Fig. 3-5b.

The instructions and questions placed in front of the mirror might read as follows:

Put your face close to these two mirrors, which are at right angles. You will see three images of your face. Two of the images appear as you normally expect they would, but what do you notice to be different about the middle image? (Answer: The middle image is upside-down.)

Wink your right eye. Which eye does your image wink? Remember, your image is upside down! Can you explain how this middle image forms? (Answers: The middle image winks its right eye. Double reflection causes the inverted image.)

Using the diagram provided, just think of one mirror in the drawing as horizontal and the other as vertical. As you can see, the middle image of the arrow is inverted.

Figure 3-6

Bending light (refraction)

This exhibit reveals what happens when light passes from air to another transparent material, such as plastic or glass. Visitors can see how light is bent (*refracted*) as it passes from air to another transparent material. Just as there is a law of reflection, so there is a law of refraction. The law of refraction is more complicated than the law of reflection, but this exhibit simply demonstrates that light bends as it enters and leaves a transparent material.

Materials
> ➤ light box (used in earlier exhibit "The law of reflection")
> ➤ clear plastic or glass block
> ➤ sheet of 8½ × 11 white paper
> ➤ 2 sheets of 8½ × 11 black construction paper

Use the same light box used for the exhibit "The law of reflection" to serve as a light source for this exhibit. (For instructions on building the light box, read the text in "The law of reflection" at the beginning of Part 3.) If the two exhibits are side by side, you can use the same box for both. Simply cut openings and prepare slitted masks for opposite sides of the box.

As before in "The law of reflection," make certain that the beam of light coming through the mask on the light box is narrow and well defined. Place the clear plastic (or glass) block on the white paper. Position the block and paper in front of the mask on the light box so that the beam of light passes through the block.

Sample instructions and questions that might accompany this exhibit are as follows:

Let the narrow beam of light from the light box enter the clear plastic (or glass) block at an angle to the surface. What happens to the light when it passes through the air into the block? (Answer: It bends.)

What happens to the light when it emerges from the plastic and enters the air? (Answer: It bends again.)

What happens if you increase the angle between the light beam and the plastic? (Answer: As the angle increases, the angle inside the block also increases.)

How do the directions of the light beam's light entering and leaving the block compare? (Answer: They appear to be parallel.)

Can you find an angle at which the light does not bend as it passes from air into the plastic block? (Answer: If the light is perpendicular to the block's surface, it does not bend.)

A convex lens and its images

A lens can produce images because it refracts (bends) light. A *convex lens* converges (brings together) parallel light rays from a distant object. The point where the parallel rays come together is called the *focal point of the lens*. The distance from the center of the lens to the focal point is called the *focal length of the lens*.

This exhibit, which focuses on how images form by convex lenses, can be built around a single light box like the one used to demonstrate reflection and refraction. Exhibit visitors will use the lens to produce an image of a picture on a slide. For instructions on building the light box, see "The law of reflection" at the beginning of Part 3. The only modification to the exhibit is that you must replace the clear bulb in the light box with an ordinary frosted bulb.

Materials
➢ light box (used in earlier exhibit "The law of reflection")
➢ frosted light bulb
➢ sheet of 8½ × 11 black construction paper
➢ dimly lit area or an area where lights can be dimmed
➢ scissors
➢ 2-inch photographic slide containing a color picture
➢ sheet of strong cardboard, appx. 1 × 2 feet
➢ sheet of 8½ × 11 white paper
➢ magnifying glass with a focal length of 10 to 20 centimeters
➢ table
➢ 3-x-5-inch file card
➢ ruler
➢ transparent tape
➢ pencil or pen

Measure and cut a hole 2 inches square in the center of the black construction paper mask on one side of the box. Tape the photographic slide over the opening.

Viewers need a screen on which to project an image. Make the screen by scoring the cardboard with the scissors and folding it in the middle. Tape the sheet of white paper on the cardboard, then place it so the paper side faces the light box. Place the white screen several feet from the light box as shown in Fig. 3-7a.

Place the magnifying glass on the table where the screen and light box rest. (You might want to chain the magnifying glass to the table.)

You can obtain a rough estimate of the focal length of the lens by taking it to another room and producing an image of a distant object seen through a window. To do this, stand near the wall opposite the

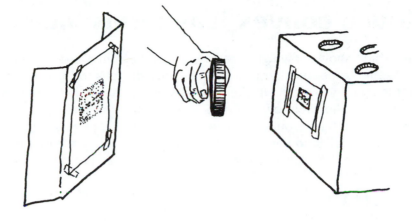

Figure 3-7a

window. Hold the lens in front of the file card and move the file card until you can see a clear image of the distant object on the card. The distance between the card and the lens is the approximate focal length of the lens. For this exhibit, a focal length between 10 and 20 centimeters will work well. Figure 3-7b shows how a convex lens bends light rays to form an image that can be seen on a screen.

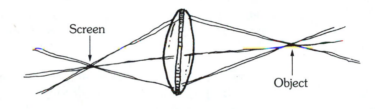

Figure 3-7b

Screen

Object

Instructions to viewers might read as follows:

Look closely at the slide that covers the illuminated opening in the box, then move the convex lens (magnifying glass) back and forth between the white screen and the illuminated slide taped to the light box until you see a sharp image on the screen. Is the image you see on the screen right-side-up or upside-down?" (Answer: It is upside-down.)

If you move the screen closer to the slide, what do you have to do to the lens to obtain a sharp image on the screen? (Answer: To get a sharp image, move the lens farther from the slide.)

If the lens is close to the slide, you cannot produce an image of the scene on the slide. Try it! Similar to the way the image of your face forms behind a mirror, the image of the scene on the slide forms behind the lens. To see the image when the lens is held close to the slide, place your eye near the lens and look through it. You can see a magnified image of the picture on the slide.

How a convex lens forms images

This exhibit shows how light beams bend as they enter and leave a lens. The beams come together at a point beyond the lens to form a one-point image. In this exhibit, the glass of water acts as a two-dimensional convex lens, showing how a convex lens produces an image. The exhibit can be built around a single light box like the one used to demonstrate reflection and refraction. For instructions on building the light box, see "The law of reflection" at the beginning of the section.

Materials

➢ light box (used in earlier exhibit "The law of reflection")
➢ heavy-duty scissors
➢ clear bulb with a straight, vertical filament
➢ sheet of 8½ × 11 black construction paper
➢ transparent tape
➢ several sheets of 8½ × 11 white paper
➢ table
➢ large diameter, clear plastic (or glass) container filled with water

The hole in the light box should be covered with a black construction mask that has near its center two narrow, vertical slits about ½ inch apart. The straight filament of the clear bulb inside the box should be parallel to the slits.

Tape several sheets of white paper to the table on which the light box rests, then place the water-filled glass on the light beams near the light box. You can see the narrow light beams bend as they enter and leave the water. The beams come together at a point on the other side of the glass (Fig. 3-8), which can be seen on the white paper resting on the table.

The information accompanying this exhibit might read as follows:

To see how a convex lens bends light to form images, look at the glass of water on the two light beams emerging from the light box. What happens to the light rays when they enter and leave the water's convex-shaped surface? Where do you see the image of the point of light? (Answers: The rays bend as they enter and leave the water's surface. The image is seen at the point where the two rays cross.)

If the same people return to this exhibit many times, you could modify it slightly by replacing the two-slit mask with a mask to which a large comb is taped. Light passing through the teeth of the comb forms many narrow beams of light. In this variation, viewers can see many light rays bend and come together at a point.

Figure 3-8

Mixing colored lights

This hands-on exhibit allows patrons to see what happens when they mix different colored lights.

Materials

➢ white wall in a darkened room or area
➢ table
➢ 1 green, 1 red, and 1 blue light bulb (25 watts each)
➢ 3 sockets with electric cords
➢ extension cord with three outlets
➢ masking tape
➢ 2, 15-x-12-inch sheets of masonite, plywood, or cardboard
➢ 2, 2-x-4-inch short pieces of lumber
➢ tablesaw or handsaw
➢ flat black paint and a paint brush
➢ copies of Figs. 3-10a and 3-10b labeled as Drawing A and Drawing B respectively
➢ electrical tape

You can purchase the colored bulbs and sockets with cords from most supermarkets or hardware stores. Low-wattage bulbs are best because they do not become hot enough to burn someone if touched.

Place the sockets with the colored light bulbs on a narrow table approximately 1 foot from the white wall. Put the blue bulb in the middle. Connect all three bulb sockets to the three-outlet extension cord, and plug the cord into an electrical outlet (Fig. 3-9a).

Because the intensity of the light from the bulbs might differ, you might need to move the bulbs slightly closer to or farther from the wall until the combined light cast on the wall is white. Once you find the right positions to produce white light, tape the sockets in place with electrical tape.

Figure 3-9a

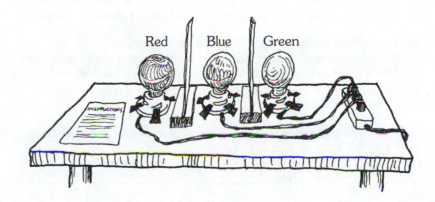
Red   Blue   Green

You will need to make two barriers to go between the bulbs. To do this, ask an adult to cut grooves in the 2 × 4s with a tablesaw or a handsaw so that the thin sheets of masonite, wood, or cardboard can fit into the grooves (Fig. 3-9b). Paint the 2 × 4s and the thin sheets with black paint to reduce the possibility of reflected colored light reaching the wall.

Figure 3-9b

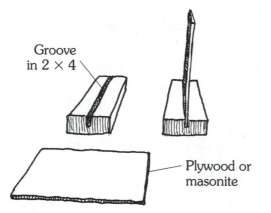

Groove in 2 × 4

Plywood or masonite

Place the barriers perpendicular to the wall between the colored lights. Provide drawings like those shown in Fig. 3-10 for your visitors as illustrations for your instructions.

Tape the sample instructions to the table between the bulbs and the edge of the table for visitors to read. The instructions might read as follows:

Push both of the vertical barriers forward so that they touch the wall and are perpendicular to it, as shown in drawing A. What color do you see on the wall between the barriers? What colors do you see on the outside of each barrier? (Answers: Blue is seen between the two barriers; red and green are seen outside the barriers.)

Pull the barrier between the blue and red bulbs back approximately 1 inch from the wall so that the blue and red light can "mix" on the wall. What color do you see where the red and blue lights mix? (Answer: Magenta—pinkish purple.)

Pull the barrier between the blue and green bulbs back approximately 1 inch from the wall so the blue and green light can "mix" on the wall. What color do you see where the green and blue lights mix? (Answer: Cyan—bluish green.)

Turn the two vertical barriers so that they form a V, as shown in drawing B. Position the apex of the V against the wall in front of the blue light to prevent blue light from reaching the wall. Now, pull the tip of the V back slightly from the wall so that red and green light can mix. What color do you see where red and green light mix? (Answer: Yellow.)

Return the vertical barriers to where they were, then pull each barrier back approximately 6 inches so that all three colored lights can shine on the wall. What is the color where red, green, and blue light mix? (Answer: White.)

Figure 3-10

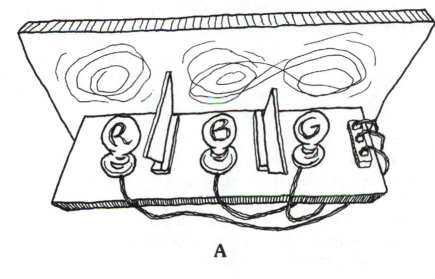

A

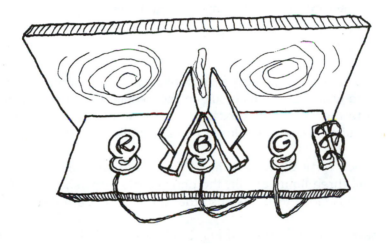

B

Colored shadows

This exhibit is a variation of the previous exhibit, "Mixing colored lights." Simply change the name of the exhibit to "Colored shadows." With just a minimal change in materials, you have a whole new exhibit.

Materials

➤ white wall in a darkened room or area
➤ table
➤ 1 green, 1 red, and 1 blue light bulb (25 watts each)
➤ 3 sockets with electric cords to fit the bulbs
➤ extension cord with three outlets
➤ pencil
➤ modeling clay
➤ barrier like the one in "Mixing colored lights"
➤ copy of Fig. 3-11
➤ electrical tape

Place the sockets with the colored light bulbs on a table about 1 foot from the white wall. Put the blue bulb in the middle. Connect all three bulb sockets to the three-outlet extension cord, and plug the cord into an electrical outlet. Tape the bulbs in place with electrical tape.

Place the pencil vertically into some of the clay and place it near the wall. When all three lights are lit, the pencil casts three shadows. Be sure the pencil is close to the wall so that the shadows are distinct.

Place the barrier and the copy of Fig. 3-11 near the bulbs.

Figure 3-11

The instructions might read as follows:

As shown in the drawing provided, use the cardboard as a screen so that only light from the green bulb reaches the pencil. How many shadows of the pencil does the green bulb cast? What is the color of the shadow? (Answers: The green bulb casts one shadow; it is black.)

Place the screen in front of the blue bulb so that both the green and red lights shine on the pencil. How many shadows of the pencil do you see? What is the color of each shadow? Why? (Answers: Two shadows are seen, one green and one red. The green light casts a red shadow because red light shines on it. The red light casts a green shadow because green light shines on it.)

Place the screen in front of the red bulb so that only the blue and green lights shine on the pencil. How many shadows of the pencil do you see? What is the color of each shadow? Why? (Answers: Two shadows are visible, one blue and one green. The blue light casts a green shadow because green light shines on it. The green light casts a blue shadow because blue light shines on it.)

Place the screen in front of the green bulb so that only the blue and red lights shine on the pencil. How many shadows of the pencil do you see? What is the color of each shadow? Why? (Answers: Two shadows are visible, one blue and one red. The blue light casts a red shadow because red light shines on it. The red light casts a blue shadow because blue light shines on it.)

Remove the screen so that all three lights shine on the pencil. How many shadows do you see? What is the color of each shadow? Why? (Answers: There are three shadows. The red light casts a cyan shadow because the blue and green lights shine on it. The green light casts a magenta shadow because the blue and red lights shine on it. The blue light casts a yellow shadow because the red and green lights shine on it.)

If you use the barrier to screen out the blue light, which shadow disappears? What happens to the other two shadows? (Answers: The yellow shadow disappears. The magenta shadow becomes red; the cyan shadow becomes green.)

If you use the barrier to screen out the green light, which shadow disappears? What happens to the other two shadows? (Answers: The magenta shadow disappears. The yellow shadow becomes red; the cyan shadow becomes blue.)

If you use the barrier to screen out the red light, which shadow disappears? What happens to the other two shadows? (Answers: The cyan shadow disappears. The magenta shadow becomes blue; the yellow shadow becomes green.)

Measuring sticks, friction, and balance

The materials for this exhibit are simple and inexpensive. Visitors will learn how friction is affected by weight and material in a surprising way. They will also see how weighting a stick affects its center of gravity or balancing point.

Materials

➤ 2 yardsticks or metersticks
➤ 3 heavy washers
➤ masking tape
➤ copy of Fig. 3-12
➤ tabletop
➤ pencil
➤ 2 self-adhesive labels

Figure 3-12

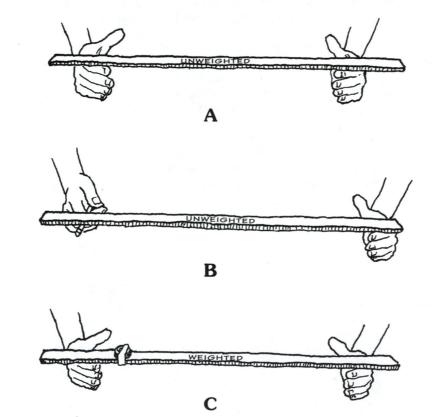

A

B

C

Label the first yardstick or meterstick "Unweighted." Tape the washers to the second yardstick or meterstick at or near the 30-inch (85-cm) line. Label that stick "Weighted." Set the materials on a tabletop and provide a copy of Fig. 3-12.

Make the instructions with the exhibit clear and easy to follow, something like the following:

Place your hands beneath the ends of the yardstick (meterstick) labeled "Unweighted," as shown in drawing A. Very slowly, move your hands closer together. Beneath what point on the stick do your hands meet?

Repeat the experiment, but this time start with one hand at the 1-inch (98-cm) line and one hand at the 24-inch (70-cm) line. Where do your hands meet this time?

Repeat the experiment again, but this time use a pencil in place of one hand as shown in drawing B. Where do your hand and the pencil meet?

Can you explain the results? (Answer: The weight of the stick is located at its center, which is its *center of gravity*, or the balance point of the stick. When you begin to move your hands together, the friction between your hands and the stick increases with weight. If more of the stick's weight is on your left hand than is on your right, then your right hand moves until the weights balance again. Conversely, if more of the stick's weight is on your right hand than is on your left, then your left hand moves until the weights balance again. Finally, both hands reach the center of the stick where its entire weight can be balanced. Although there is less friction between the pencil and the yardstick than between your hand and the yardstick, the same principle applies and the results are the same.)

Repeat the experiment once more. This time use the stick labeled "Weighted," as shown in drawing C. Where do your hands meet this time? Can you explain the results? (Answer: With a weighted stick, the center of gravity is not at the center; it is closer to the weighted end. The point where your hands meet is the weighted stick's center of gravity.)

A question of balance

This exhibit provides a puzzle that involves both Archimedes' principle and Newton's law. Archimedes' principle tells us that a body in water is buoyed upward by a force equal to the weight of the water displaced. Newton's third law states that if one body exerts a force on a second body, the second body exerts an equal but oppositely directed force on the first.

Materials

➢ Harvard trip balance
➢ 2 large and 1 small beaker
➢ water
➢ eyedropper
➢ tabletop
➢ paper towels

Fill the two large beakers with water so that both beakers contain equal amounts. Place the two beakers onto the balance, one on each pan (Fig. 3-13). Fill the small beaker with water and place it next to the balance along with the eyedropper and paper towels.

Figure 3-13

The information provided to your patrons and the questions asked of them should be similar to the following:

The weights of the two beakers of water on this balance should be equal. If they are not, use the eyedropper to add water to the lighter beaker until the weights are equal.

Now try to answer this question: If you dip your fingers into the water in one of the beakers without touching the beaker itself, does the beam remain balanced? If your answer is "no," which beaker do you predict will be heavier?

Now test your prediction by dipping one or more fingers of one hand into the water in one of the beakers. Did you predict correctly? Explain the result of your experiment. (Answer: The beaker into which you dip your fingers is heavier. When you dip your fingers into the beaker, you displace some water. A force equal to the weight of the displaced water buoys your fingers upward. An equal force is exerted downward on the water. That downward force pushes on the balance pan.)

A weighing question

Visitors engaged by this "feet-on" exhibit will learn that their total weight remains the same regardless of how it is distributed.

Materials

➤ 2 bathroom scales
➤ poster board
➤ easel to display board or thumbtacks or heavy-duty tape to hang board on wall

Place the bathroom scales on the floor in front of a large sign made from the poster board.

Your sign should contain the following information and questions:

How much do you weigh? Step on one of these scales and find out. How much do you weigh when you stand on the scale on one foot? (Answer: Your weight remains unchanged.)

Stand with one foot on each of the scales at the same time. What does each scale read? (Answer: If your weight is equally distributed, each scale shows half your weight. If you place more weight on one foot than on the other, the sum of the two weighings equals your weight.)

If the scales are sturdy, you might add the following question:

What does each scale read when you put one scale on top of the other and then stand on the top scale? (Answer: The reading on the top scale is your weight. The reading on the bottom scale is your weight plus the weight of the scale on which you are standing.)

Pendulums

For many years, the pendulum clock was the world's most accurate timepiece. Though pendulum clocks are still accurate, the pendulums used today are more subtle. Today's pendulums appear in the form of a crystal in quartz watches and as oscillating electric and magnetic fields in atomic clocks, but we still use carefully constructed pendulums to measure the strength of gravity at different places on the earth's surface.

In this exhibit, hands-on experimenters have an opportunity to see how amplitude, length, and the weight of the bob affect the period of a pendulum. A *period* is the time it takes for the pendulum bob to make one complete swing. If your exhibits are in a school, you might be able to borrow ring stands and clamps from the science department. If you cannot borrow the necessary equipment, you need to construct your own pendulum supports from lumber.

Materials

➤ lightweight fishing line
➤ 8 metal balls with hooks or 8 steel washers (2 should be of a different weight)
➤ ring stands and pendulum clamps borrowed from a school laboratory: 8 C-clamps: 2, 4-inch clamps and 6, 2-inch clamps
➤ 2 C-clamps
➤ clock with a second hand
➤ metric ruler
➤ lumber to build frame from which to suspend pendulums, 2 × 4s and 1 × 2s
➤ scissors
➤ tabletop

This experiment requires the use of three different sets of pendulums (Fig. 3-14). The first two sets each contain two pendulums; the third set contains three pendulums.

Figure 3-14

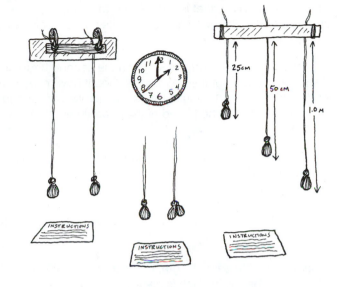

You are going to make the first pair of pendulums exactly the same length. A length of 1 meter gives the pendulums a period of almost exactly 2 seconds. When measuring the lengths of the pendulums, measure from the point of support to the middle of the bob.

Measure and cut the fishing line. Tie one end of the fishing line to the bob by threading it through the hook or the eyelet. Put the other end of the line between a pendulum clamp or two boards. If you use boards, clamp them firmly together with C-clamps. Adjust the length by loosening the clamps and pulling the line up or down until you attain the desired length.

Make the second pair of pendulums equal in length also but use bobs with different weights. You could use a lead ball as one bob and a steel ball of the same diameter for the other bob, or you could hang a one-washer bob on one pendulum and a two-washer bob on the other.

In the third set of pendulums, which is the set of three, the first pendulum is 25 centimeters long, the second is 50 centimeters long, and the third is 100 centimeters in length. The bobs are identical.

Place a clock with a second hand near the pendulums so experimenters can measure the periods of the pendulums.

The instructions at the base of the first pair of pendulums might read as follows:

These two pendulums are both 1 meter long, and both bobs have the same weight. Pull one pendulum bob back about 2 centimeters; pull the other back about 4 centimeters. Try to release both at the same time. How do the periods of these two pendulums compare? (A *period* is the time it takes for the pendulum bob to make one complete swing; that is, for the bob to swing from the point of release to the opposite end of its swing and back to its release point again.) (Answer: The periods are the same.)

To find the actual period of these pendulums, watch the second hand on the clock as you release one or both of the pendulums. Count how many complete swings each pendulum makes in 1 minute. Divide the number of seconds (60) by the number of swings. What is the period of the pendulum(s)? (Answer: The period is 2 seconds.)

From what you have seen, how does the amplitude of the pendulum (the length of its swing) affect its period? (Answer: The amplitude does not affect the period.)

The instructions for the second pair of pendulums might read like the following:

These two pendulums have the same length, but one bob weighs more than the other. Gently lift the two bobs. Which bob is heavier? To see what effect the weight of a bob has on the period of a pendulum, pull both bobs back about 2 centimeters and release them. How do the periods of the two pendulums compare? How does the bob's weight affect the period of a pendulum? (Answers: The periods are the same. The bob's weight does not affect the period.)

Here are the instructions you might use for the third set of pendulums:

These three pendulums are 25, 50, and 100 centimeters long. Measure the period of each pendulum by counting the number of complete swings the pendulum makes in 1 minute. What is the period of each pendulum? Does the period of a pendulum double when its length doubles? Does the period of a pendulum double when its length quadruples? (Answers: The periods are very close to 1 second, 1.4 seconds, and 2 seconds. The period does not double when the length doubles; it does double when the length quadruples.)

Coupled pendulums

This exhibit can serve as a sequel to the "Pendulums" exhibit. It demonstrates the transfer of energy between moving pendulums.

Materials

➤ lightweight fishing line
➤ 2 lead sinkers
➤ drinking straw or a thin stick
➤ ring stands and pendulum clamp or pendulum frame like the one used in the previous exhibit
➤ 2, 2-inch C-clamps
➤ metric ruler
➤ scissors
➤ tabletop

To build your coupled pendulums, tie each lead sinker onto the ends of two pieces of fishing line, each 40 centimeters long. The sinkers serve as the bobs of the pendulums. Place the two pendulums about 15 centimeters apart, and suspend them as in the previous exhibit "Pendulums." Be sure the pendulums are of equal length.

Connect the two pendulums at a point about 15 centimeters above the bobs with a drinking straw or a thin stick as shown in Fig. 3-15. Simply loop each string once around the straw or stick.

Figure 3-15

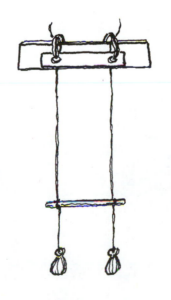

Instructions to the experimenters might be written as follows:

These two pendulums are connected and are called *coupled pendulums*. Pull one of the bobs a short distance to one side and release it. Then watch. What happens? Can you explain why it happens? (Answers: The back-and-forth motion of the pendulum gradually decreases and finally stops. Meanwhile, the motion of the second pendulum gradually increases. Then the motion of the second pendulum transfers back to the first one. The transfer of energy takes place because the moving pendulum tugs on the stationary pendulum through the straw and the stationary one tugs back. The timing of the tugs is such that the motion of one pendulum always increases at the expense of the other.

You might extend this exhibit by asking how moving the connecting stick closer to the bobs affects the pendulums' behavior or what effect changing the length of the pendulums has on their motion.

Tornado bottles

This inexpensive exhibit demonstrates in miniature the funnel of rotating air that constitutes a tornado, although the forces here are different from the forces that give rise to a tornado. Your visitors will also enjoy watching the swirling water as it flows from the upper to the lower bottle.

Materials

➤ 2 clear 1-liter plastic soda bottles
➤ water
➤ food coloring
➤ paper towel
➤ masking tape or duct tape

Remove any labels from the soda bottles. Fill one of the bottles half full with water and add a drop or two of food coloring. Dry the mouths of both bottles with a paper towel.

Turn the empty bottle upside down and put its mouth against the mouth of the bottle that contains the colored water. Seal the mouths and necks of the two bottles together with tape (Fig. 3-16a).

Turn the bottles over so that the bottle with water is on top. Grasp the necks of the bottles and swirl the bottles in a couple of small tight circles (Fig. 3-16b). This motion makes the water in the upper bottle swirl against the outside of the bottle, leaving an air space in the center as gravity pulls the water downward (Fig. 3-16c).

Figure 3-16

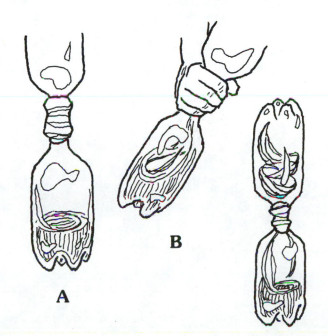

A

B

C

The flow of water from the upper to the lower bottle resembles a tornado. Actually the forces here are different than those of a tornado, but this is a good demonstration of the funnel of rotating air that constitutes a tornado.

All you need is a few words of introduction, such as the following:

Turn these bottles upside down. Quickly swirl the water in the upper bottle and watch the "tornado" that forms. What forces do you think are involved in making this tornado?" (Answers will vary but some may say that centrifugal force keeps the swirling water against the wall of the bottle, leaving air at the bottle's central axis.)

Sound, vibration, and music

In this exhibit, visitors discover that the frequency of a vibration is related to the pitch of the sound it makes and to the length of the object that is vibrating. Visitors then conduct experiments to see how the tension and thickness of a string affect its pitch.

Materials

➢ 3 plastic or wooden rulers
➢ table
➢ 2 C-clamps
➢ 1-foot-long piece of wood, any width
➢ 30-inch-long piece of 10-pound fishing line (or piano wire)
➢ 3, 30-inch-long pieces of 50-pound fishing line (or piano wire)
➢ 2 boards, appx. 6 inches wide, 2 feet long, and ½ inch thick
➢ 4 nails
➢ hammer
➢ 2 pencils
➢ 4 small plastic pails
➢ sand
➢ measuring cup

This exhibit is divided into two parts. For the first part, clamp the three rulers to the edge of the table with the 1-foot-long piece of wood and the C-clamps as shown in Fig. 3-17. Extend one ruler far enough from the edge so that its up-and-down vibration is easily seen when it is plucked. Extend the second ruler a shorter distance from the edge so that its vibration is more rapid and the sound it produces has a higher pitch. Set the third ruler so that it has an even shorter length; its vibration is more rapid, and its pitch higher still.

You might have to adjust the lengths of the rulers beyond the clamp until you obtain the appropriate vibrations and pitches.

Figure 3-17

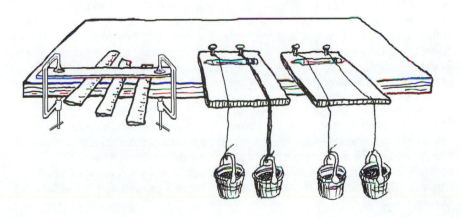

Your exhibit card should be set near the rulers and should contain instructions similar to the following:

When things vibrate, they produce sounds. You can make sounds by gently plucking the ends of each of these three rulers in turn. Which ruler vibrates slowest? Which vibrates fastest? Which one makes the lowest pitched sound? Which one makes the highest pitched sound? (Answers: The longest ruler vibrates with the lowest frequency and has the lowest pitch. The shortest ruler vibrates with the highest frequency and has the highest pitch.)

For the second part of this exhibit, have an adult hammer two nails into one end of each of the two 6-inch boards. The nails should enter the boards and not the tabletop. Place the two boards on the table. The ends without nails should project no more than 1 inch beyond the edge of the table.

To see how the thickness of a string affects its pitch, attach two different fishing lines, one 10-pound and one 50-pound or two piano wires of different thicknesses to the nails at one end of one of the boards (Fig. 3-17). Place a pencil under the strings near the nails to keep the strings off the board so they are free to vibrate.

Tie a plastic pail to the end of each string and fill the pails with equal amounts of sand so that both strings have the same amount of tension. The pails should hang over the edge of the board and table.

On the second 6-inch-wide board, attach the remaining two 50-pound lines to the nails just as you did with the first board. Tie the remaining two pails to these strings. Put a pencil beneath the strings just as you did with the first board. This time, put more sand in one pail than in the other so that the tension on one string is greater than on the other. Place this board next to the other, perpendicular to the table's edge.

The following information/instructions might be placed between the two boards:

Now you can discover how the thickness of a string affects its pitch. The board on your left supports two strings of different thicknesses. The tension on the wires, which is supplied by the pails of sand, is the same. The lengths of the strings between the pencil and the end of the board is the same. In turn, pluck each string between the pencil and the end of the board where the string is free to vibrate. Which string has the higher pitch? Can you tell by listening, which one vibrates at a lower frequency? (Answer: The thicker string makes a lower pitch and therefore, vibrates at a lower frequency.)

Move the pencil further down the string, away from the nails, to shorten the length of the string between the pencil and the end of the board. Pluck the strings again. Then return the pencil to its original position. How does shortening the length of a string affect the pitch of the sound it produces? (Answer: Shortening the length of the string increases the pitch of the sound it makes.)

The strings on the board on the right are of equal thickness and length. However, as you can see by looking into the pails, the tension on one string is greater than the tension on the other. Pluck both strings. How does tension affect the pitch of the sound made by the vibrating string? How does tension affect the string's frequency of vibration? (Answers: The pitch, or frequency of vibration, becomes higher when the tension on the string is greater.)

Other ideas for exhibits

➤ Show how a concave lens diverges (spreads) light and produces images that make things appear smaller.

➤ Fill bottles with thick, colored liquids that form slow-moving waves when tipped. You can find models for these "wave bottles" in many gift shops and variety stores.

➤ Make some simple musical instruments that people can play (Fig. 3-18):
  • Fill some glass beakers of different sizes with varying amounts of water to create an octave of notes.
  • Create an instrument similar to the beakers by hanging clean, unglazed, earthenware flowerpots of different sizes from strong strings.
  • Make metal chimes from electrical conduit tubing cut to different lengths.
  • Use a wooden block and C-clamps to fix tongue depressors to a table. Let the depressors extend different distances from the edge of the table.
  • Make a one-stringed banjo on which you can play different notes by changing the length of the vibrating string.

➤ Set up an exhibit that allows visitors to measure the wavelength of sound.

➤ When humidity is minimal, build an exhibit that allows people to do simple experiments dealing with static electricity.

Figure 3-18

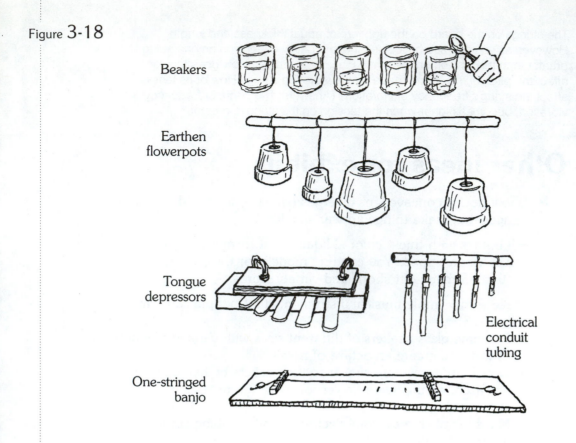

Beakers

Earthen
flowerpots

Tongue
depressors

Electrical
conduit
tubing

One-stringed
banjo

Part 4

Optical mysteries and other puzzles

People enjoy puzzles, illusions, and mind teasers. Consequently, you might find some of the exhibits in this section to be the most popular in your museum. Puzzles encourage people to use their analytical abilities, sometimes to test their senses, and to challenge their ideas.

Is seeing believing?

Most people enjoy illusions. They never seem to tire of being fooled
by their senses. Psychological and physiological explanations of
illusions are interesting, but you will often find disagreement among
those who attempt to explain illusions.

Materials

➤ copy of Fig. 4-1
➤ ruler

Figure 4-1 shows some of the puzzles you might display in an exhibit
on illusions. You can find or create many more illusions and enlarge
them with a photocopier to present at this exhibit.

In addition to the illusions and the instructions or explanations on
your exhibit card, provide visitors with a ruler so they can resolve for
themselves the questions posed about lines in the illusions.

The copy of Fig. 4-1 can be used as questions to accompany the
illusions. The answers can be readily attained by using a ruler.

Figure 4-1

Which of the
two horizontal
lines is longer?

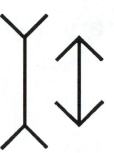

Which of the
vertical lines
is longer?

Which line is longer?
The one to the left
of the dot, or the one
to the right of the dot?

Is the diagonal line
that is entering and
leaving the vertical lines
a straight line?

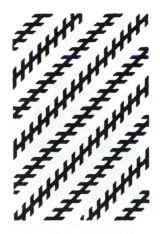

Are these diagonal
lines parallel?

Which line appears to be longer?

Mystery objects

In an effort to teach visitors some of the tools used in scientific experimentation, you can set up a table or booth in your museum to display various mystery objects.

Materials

➤ slips of paper
➤ pencils
➤ shoebox with a slit cut in the top
➤ various objects used in science experiments or photographs or illustrations of these objects
➤ tabletop

This exhibit is actually a contest in which you present a new mystery object or photograph each week. Invite viewers to write down what they think an object is on a sheet of paper and to place their responses in a slotted box. Each week, announce a winner, if there is one, and the correct answer. At the same time, replace the old mystery objects with new ones.

You can display science equipment such as a mortar and pestle, a petri dish, a burette clamp, a Bunsen burner, and so on. However, your contest doesn't have to be limited to scientific objects. You can also display mystery objects that are tools or kitchen items no longer in everyday use, such as ice tongs (used to carry blocks of ice), a froe (used to cut wood into shingles), a washboard (for scrubbing clothes), a scythe (to cut tall grass), a coffee grinder (to grind coffee beans), and so on.

If you have a flair for photography, you might display mystery photos and ask people if they can identify the object in the picture. For example, you might present photographs of some of the mystery objects mentioned above, or you could take close-up photographs of such common things as door mats, asphalt, dried mud, a furnace filter, the air bubbles in ice, and so on.

Leonardo's notes

Leonardo daVinci (1452–1519) was a great Renaissance man who excelled as an artist and who, as a scientist, was often ahead of his time. His well-known paintings include the Mona Lisa and the Last Supper. His work in science, which reveals his skills as an inventor, architect, astronomer, biologist, and mathematician, was not recognized until his notes were discovered in old libraries. Leonardo did not want to share his scientific ideas with others. In order to keep his ideas to himself, he wrote his notes in a form known as *mirror writing* (Fig. 4-2). Leonardo's mirror writing forms the basis of this exhibit.

Figure 4-2

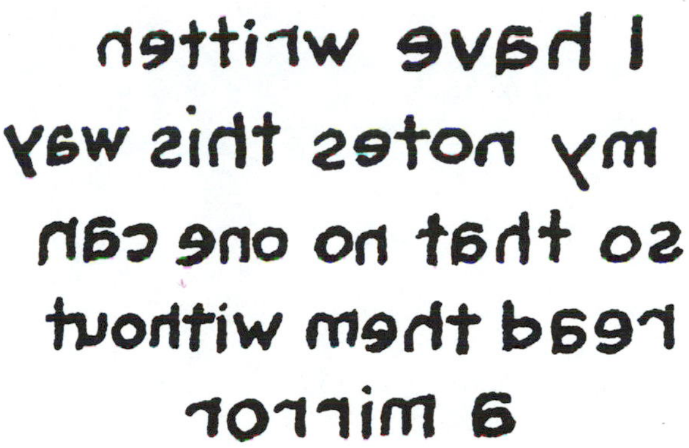

Materials
- ➤ copy of Fig. 4-2
- ➤ wall or sheet of cardboard, appx. 11 × 17 inches
- ➤ transparent tape
- ➤ notepad
- ➤ pencil
- ➤ metallic or plastic mirror

Tape the copy of Fig. 4-2 upright on a wall or use the cardboard as a screen together with your exhibit instructions.

Visitors use the mirror to test their proposed solutions for reading Leonardo's notes.

Your visitors should find instructions similar to the following placed with your diagram:

Leonardo daVinci (1452–1519) was well known as an artist (he painted the Mona Lisa), but he was also an extremely competent scientist, inventor, and engineer. To keep his scientific ideas secret, he wrote his notes in a code that others could not read. Had Leonardo written his notes in English, they might have looked something like the figure displayed here. Can you find a way to read these notes? What do they say? (Answers: You can read the notes by looking into a mirror held in front of the figure. The notes read as follows: I have written my notes in this way so that no one can read them without a mirror.)

In the second part of this exhibit, visitors will need the notepad, pencil, and the mirror. Invite them to write their names in mirror writing so that they can read their names in the mirror.

A burning, underwater candle

Viewers will be amazed to see a candle burning inside a large, water-filled beaker or jar. As the exhibitor, you know perfectly well that a candle cannot burn in water, but by using a well-known law of reflection you can produce an *image* of a candle that appears to be burning under water.

Materials

➢ table
➢ darkened room or area
➢ matches
➢ short candle
➢ candle holder
➢ 1-foot-square sheet of window glass
➢ masking tape
➢ 4 bricks
➢ large beaker or glass jar
➢ water
➢ nonreflective pie tin or pan
➢ copy of Fig. 4-3
➢ modeling clay or bricks
➢ ruler

Figure 4-3

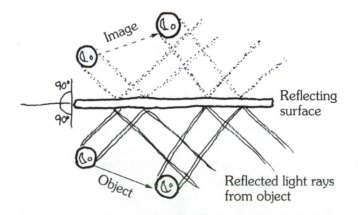

 Because you will be using matches and a burning candle, *ask an adult to help you set up this exhibit.* The exhibit is most effective in a dark area where only light from the burning candle reaches the reflecting surface. The glass surface reflects enough light so that an image of the candle and flame is clearly visible. No light should come from the back side of the glass. Such light would reduce the contrast between the image and its background.

Together with an adult, obtain a 1-foot-square sheet of window glass from a hardware store. Someone there can cut the glass for you. Cover the edges of the glass with masking tape to prevent cuts. Clean the glass thoroughly, then set it upright on a table using the bricks to support the glass (Fig. 4-4).

Figure 4-4

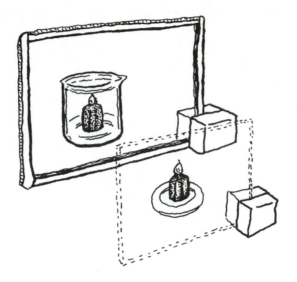

Set the candle firmly into the candle holder and place it approximately 6 inches in front of the vertical sheet of glass. (You can substitute an alcohol burner or a Bunsen burner [if gas is available] at your exhibit in place of the candle.)

Place the large, water-filled beaker or jar 6 inches behind the glass along a line perpendicular to the glass that connects the candle and the beaker. You should now see the image of the candle in the center of the beaker.

Because you want exhibit viewers to think the flame is under water, you must hide the candle from their line of sight. Shield the candle from view with the dark pie tin or pan. The pan can be supported upright by two bricks. Don't use a shiny pan because it will reflect light; dark metal reflects little light and provides a safe, nonflammable barrier between the flame and the viewer.

Even though the candle is in a holder, do not leave an open flame unattended. This exhibit should only be open when someone is nearby to oversee it. In addition, if you use the candle instead of an alcohol burner or Bunsen burner, the candle will have to be replaced quite often.

Place a diagram of Fig. 4-3 nearby. Instructions to your viewers might read as follows:

This candle appears to be burning under water. Can a candle really burn under water? How can you explain what you see? (Answers: No, a candle cannot burn under water. What is seen is an image of a candle reflected by the clear glass in front of it. The candle, which is in front of the glass, is hidden by the pan. The image, like all images seen in plane (flat) reflecting surfaces is as far behind the mirror as the candle is in front of it. [See diagram that explains how images are formed.])

This exhibit might serve well at your museum's opening night (or day). It can then be replaced with another more permanent exhibit requiring a dark environment, such as the following exhibit.

The little bulb that isn't there

In this exhibit, viewers will look at and attempt to touch what appears to be a glowing bulb inside a small hole. When they try to touch the bulb, they discover the bulb isn't really there.

What your visitors see and try to touch is an *image* of a flashlight bulb, which is produced by a concave (saucer-shaped) mirror. This image is not like the images seen in plane (flat) mirrors. Plane mirrors produce an image that appears to be behind the mirror. The image produced by the concave mirror really is where it appears to be.

Materials

- concave mirror with a focal length of 15 to 25 centimeters[1]
- cardboard or boards to make a long (appx. 1 foot) thin (appx. 6 × 6 inches) box
- 1 threaded flashlight bulb
- 2 threaded sockets for bulb (sockets with two screw holes on their base)
- 1 or 2 D-cell batteries
- battery holder
- 2 insulated wires, appx. 6 inches long
- duct tape
- modeling clay
- 3-x-5-inch file card
- tape measure
- heavy-duty scissors
- wood or cardboard shelf, appx. 3 inches wide
- screwdriver
- drill
- copies of Figs. 4-6a, b, c & d

You need to put together a cardboard or wooden box like the one shown in Fig. 4-5. The inside length of the box should be several centimeters longer than twice the focal length of the mirror you are using. The height of the box should be several centimeters greater than twice the height of the flashlight bulb and the socket. The width of the box should accommodate the flashlight batteries, battery holder(s), and wires without them interfering with the light path between the bulb, the mirror, and the image.

---

1 To find the focal length of your concave mirror, stand on the side of an unlighted room opposite a window. Turn the mirror toward a distant object that you can see through the window. Have someone move a screen—a white file card works well—back and forth in front of the mirror until you can see a clear image of the distant object on the card. The distance between the mirror and the card is very nearly the focal length.

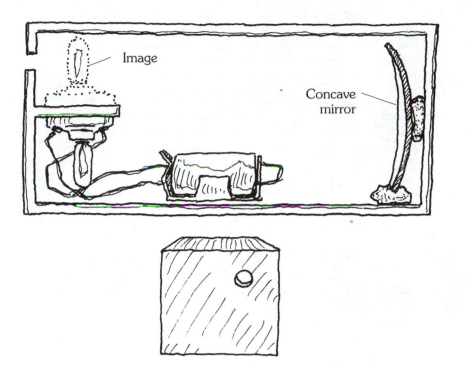

Figure 4-5

You might have to experiment to find out how many batteries (1 or 2 will probably suffice) you need to light the bulb. The bulb should glow brightly but not so bright that it burns out after a short time.

On the viewing end of the box, you will need to add the shelf as shown in Fig. 4-5. If you use wood, you can tack or glue the shelf in place. If you use cardboard, make the shelf by folding a piece of cardboard and taping it in place. Screw or tape one of the empty sockets onto the top of the shelf. Screw or tape the other empty socket on the bottom of the shelf.

 Have an adult drill or cut a viewing hole about 1 inch in diameter at the end of the box where the image will appear. The hole should be in line with and just above the socket so that people can see and attempt to touch the "bulb that isn't there."

Position the mirror exactly two focal lengths from the bulb and sockets. At that distance, the image of the inverted bulb will appear right-side-up in the empty socket directly above the lighted bulb beneath the shelf. Use the file card to locate the image while you are adjusting the mirror to ensure that the image appears to be in the upper socket. Affix the mirror in place with the clay.

Once the image is properly positioned, place the top on the box and tape it shut. If the box is made of wood, you can add hinges and locks to the lid, but you won't need these unless people persist in removing the tape and opening the box. You might prevent this problem and relieve their curiosity by promising to open the box and reveal the secret at a later time or you can provide diagrams and an explanation with the exhibit. Use diagrams similar to those shown in Fig. 4-6.

Figure 4-6

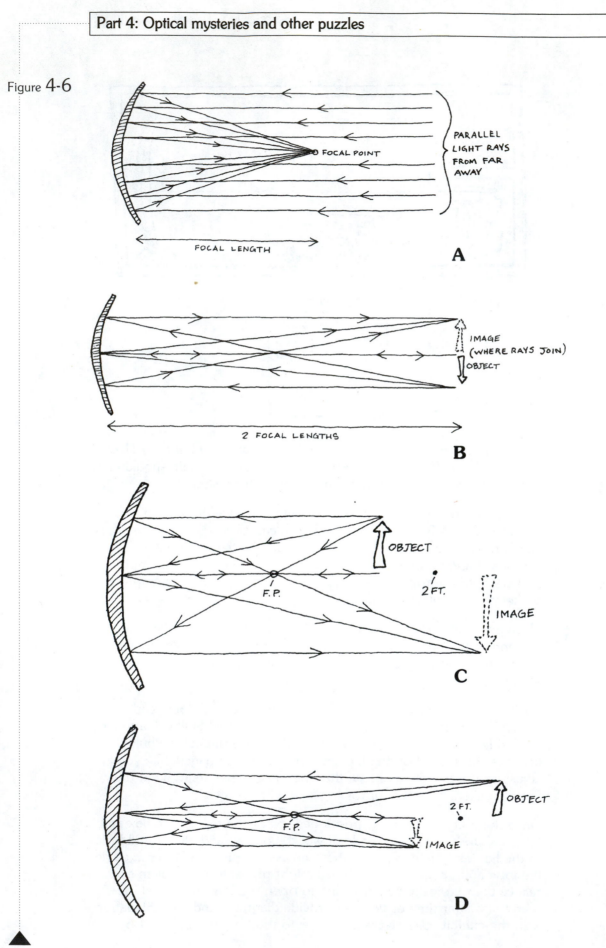

The card beside the exhibit might read like the following:

Look through the hole at the end of this box. See a glowing flashlight bulb? This is the little bulb that isn't there. To see that the bulb isn't really there, put your finger through the hole and try to touch the bulb. You can feel the bulb's socket beneath the hole, but the bulb isn't there. Can you explain where it is?

(Answer: A concave mirror at the other end of the box produces an image in front of the mirror because that is where light rays from the bulb that are reflected by the mirror actually come together to form an image of the bulb. A concave mirror *converges* (brings together) parallel light. If the rays are parallel they all converge at a single point, called the *focal point* of the mirror. The *focal length* of a concave mirror is the distance between the mirror and its focal point (see diagram A).

The images seen in plane mirrors are called *virtual images*. They exist only because the divergence (spreading out) of light rays reflected from a flat surface makes the rays appear to be coming from behind the mirror. Try as you might, you cannot "capture" a virtual image on a screen.

On the other hand, the image produced in front of a concave mirror is really there. That might be why it is called a *real image*. You can see a real image on a screen held at the place where the light rays come together. In the diagrams provided, B, the object is two focal lengths from the concave mirror. As you can see, its image is also two focal lengths in front of the mirror and the same size as the object.)

Diagram C shows that if the object is less than two focal lengths from the mirror, its image appears to be larger than the object and more than two focal lengths in front of the mirror. In image D, the object is more than two focal lengths from the mirror and its image appears smaller than the object and forms between the object and the mirror.

If an object is two focal lengths in front of a concave mirror, the image of the object forms the same distance from the mirror (two focal lengths). Knowing the focal length of the concave mirror is useful in setting up this exhibit.

Inverted words and cylindrical lenses

A cylinder-shaped lens will bend light but not in three dimensions the way an ordinary (spherical) lens will. Consequently, its images, if upside-down, will not be reversed right for left. Or, if turned right for left, the image will not be inverted. In this exhibit, viewers will have an opportunity to see images formed by cylindrical lenses while being teased with a suggestion that image inversion is caused by the color of the lens.

Materials

> ➤ 2 large test tubes or plastic vials
> ➤ 2 stoppers, corks, or caps for the tubes or vials
> ➤ warm water
> ➤ blue and red food coloring
> ➤ 2 sheets of paper
> ➤ pencil
> ➤ clay

Fill the two test tubes or plastic vials with warm water. The reason for using warm water is to be sure that air bubbles do not appear. Air dissolved in cold water can form bubbles as it warms.

Add a few drops of blue food coloring to one test tube or vial and a few drops of red food coloring to the other test tube or vial. Add enough food coloring so that the liquid in the tube is distinctly blue or red but sufficiently diluted so that you can see through it. Use the stoppers, corks, or caps to seal both tubes or vials. Make certain that no bubbles obscure your view through the tubes.

On one sheet of paper write the word "CHOICE." On the second sheet of paper, write the word "MUSEUM." Be sure the words are smaller than the "lenses," or tubes or vials. Place the tube filled with red liquid over the word "MUSEUM." Looking down on the paper through the tube, raise the tube toward you until the word appears inverted. Then affix the tube in this position by supporting it with clay at each end (Fig. 4-7).

Place the tube filled with blue liquid over the word CHOICE. Support it at the same height above the word as you did the other tube. This time the word does not appear to be inverted.

Figure 4-7

The exhibit card might read like the following:

The word *MUSEUM* lies beneath the red cylindrical lens. The word *CHOICE* lies beneath the blue cylindrical lens. Why does the word beneath the red liquid appear to be upside-down while the word beneath the blue liquid appears to be right-side-up? (Answer: Both words have been inverted, but inverting the letters in *CHOICE* has no effect on their appearance. Each of the letters used in the word *CHOICE* appears the same regardless of whether you see them right-side-up or upside-down.)

How thick is a page in a book?

Viewers of this exhibit will learn that they can make an accurate estimate of the thickness of a page in a book, something that is far too small to measure with a ruler. The key is to measure many identical pages. Dividing the thickness of many pages by the number of pages provides a reasonable estimate of the thickness of a single page.

Materials

➢ 2 C-clamps
➢ book
➢ plastic ruler

Stand the book on its end (the bound backing) and use the two C-clamps to support the book firmly without excessive squeezing (Fig. 4-8). Place a ruler across the pages to measure the thickness of all the pages in the book.

Figure 4-8

The information and questions for viewers might read like the following:

There are X pages between the covers of this book. Use the ruler to find the thickness of all the pages. How thick is a single sheet? (Remember each sheet is two pages!) (Answer: X/thickness. If there are 400 pages and they are 3 centimeters thick, then the answer would be 3 centimeters/200 sheets = 0.015 centimeter, or 0.15 millimeter.)

What makes a drinking bird drink?

In this exhibit, visitors observe a toy bird that seems to be drinking water from a cup or beaker. The natural question that arises as one watches such a bird is: What makes the bird drink? It certainly isn't thirsty!

Materials

➤ drinking bird (sometimes called a dipping bird)
➤ water
➤ cup or beaker
➤ clock with a second hand
➤ notepad
➤ shoebox
➤ pencil or pen
➤ tabletop
➤ electric fan
➤ scissors

You can buy a drinking bird (Fig. 4-9) in many novelty stores. To make the bird begin to dip, wet its head with water.

Figure 4-9

This exhibit is divided into three phases.

For the first phase, place the cup or beaker filled with water in such a position that the bird's beak dips into the liquid when its head comes down. Once the bird starts "drinking," it will continue to "drink" for as long as you supply it with water.

Initially, simply display the drinking bird engaged in its favorite activity, provide a clock with a second hand, and two very general questions on an exhibit card:

What causes this bird to drink? (Answer: As water evaporates from the bird's cloth-covered head, the cloth cools because evaporation absorbs heat. Heat then flows from the gas inside the glass bulb to the cooler cloth that surrounds it. As the gas cools, its pressure drops. The pressure in the bulb near the bird's tail is now greater than the pressure in the upper bulb. This forces liquid up the tube that connects the lower bulb with the upper bulb in the bird's head. As the liquid rises, the weight of the bird's head increases. Finally, the increase in weight makes the bird dip and "drink." When the bird dips, the lower end of the tube emerges from the liquid and the liquid falls back into the lower bulb. This shifts weight back to the bird's tail causing the bulb at the bird's tail to fall and the bird's head to rise.)

How many times does the bird "drink" each minute? (Answer: The answer to this question depends on the conditions around the bird, but it can be found by simply counting the number of times the bird dips into the water in one or more minutes. Humidity is the major factor affecting the bird's drinking rate. High humidity, which causes evaporation to diminish, reduces the bird's drinking rate.)

Once visitors are familiar with the bird, move to the second phase of the exhibit. Cut a slit in the top of the shoebox. Place the notepad, the pencil or pen, and the box beside the exhibit and post another question:

What do you think will happen to the bird's drinking rate if we blow air across its head with a fan? Drop your answers into the box provided. Return on (give a date) to see if you were right.

For the third phase of the exhibit, paraphrase and post a list of some or all of the answers you received. Then use a fan to produce a *gentle* breeze across the bird's head and ask:

What effect does the breeze have on the bird's drinking rate? Can you explain why? (Answers: The breeze has increased the bird's drinking rate. The breeze increases the rate at which water evaporates.)

A gravity-defying hammer

Your center of gravity—the point where all your weight can be considered to be located—is several inches below your navel. If you lie across a rail fence with your center of gravity on the rail, your body will balance. In some cases, the center of gravity of an object is outside of the actual object. For example, the center of gravity of a metal washer is at the center of the washer where there is no metal. The center of gravity of the hammer used in this exhibit is located in a position where it does not cause the ruler to which it is attached to rotate.

Materials

- ➤ hammer
- ➤ strong rubber band
- ➤ sturdy ruler
- ➤ table or shelf

Use the hammer, the rubber band, and the sturdy ruler to build the exhibit shown in Fig. 4-10. Because visitors might want to touch the hammer, which would destroy the sensitive balance, you should place this exhibit in an enclosed display or out of reach so it is not disturbed.

Figure 4-10

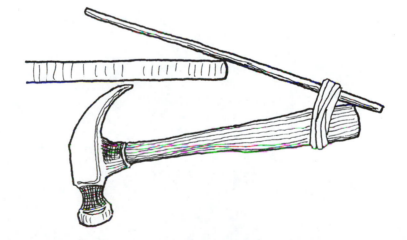

The following question might accompany the exhibit:

Why doesn't this hammer and ruler fall off the table? (Answer: The center of gravity of the hammer and ruler is under the table. Therefore, there is no force beyond the point of support to rotate the ruler off the table.)

You might also suggest an experiment related to a person's own center of gravity that people can try at any nearby wall:

If you stand with your left shoulder, side, and foot against a wall, you cannot lift your right foot. The reason is that your center of gravity is near the center of your body. If you lift your right foot, your center of gravity where all your weight is considered to be located, is beyond your only point of support (your left foot).

If you move away from the wall, you can lift your right foot without difficulty. The reason is that you automatically tilt your body to the left so that your center of gravity is placed above your left foot. With the wall against your side, you cannot tilt your body and move your center of gravity.

Your blind spot

In this exhibit, your visitors will enjoy discovering their own blind spot.

Materials

➤ copy of Fig. 4-11
➤ transparent tape

●

Figure 4-11

Provide a copy of Fig. 4-11 for your visitors along with the following instructions:

Look closely at the paper taped to the wall (or other location). It consists of a dot on the left and an X on the right that are about 3 inches apart. Close your left eye and stare at the dot with your right eye as you slowly move your head closer and closer to the dot. You will find a point where the X disappears. Does the X reappear as you move your head still closer to the dot? (Answer: Yes.)

Repeat the experiment with your right eye closed, but this time stare at the X as you move your head closer to the X. Can you find a point where the dot disappears? (Answer: Yes.)

All of us have a spot in our eye where we cannot see. In a small area at the back of your eye where the nerve cells of the retina join to form the optic nerve that leads to the back of the brain, there are no nerve cells that respond to light. If an image falls on that small area, known as the *blind spot*, you cannot detect it.

You could enhance the exhibit by finding and posting a colored, labeled drawing of the human eye. Indicate to viewers that segment of the picture that shows where the optic nerve joins the retina.

Trick photography

Photographs can sometimes create their own optical illusions. Visitors at this exhibit will enjoy seeing someone holding two small people on his or her hands and seeing someone else suspended in midair.

Materials
➤ several friends
➤ camera and film
➤ full-length mirror or window

Photograph a person with his or her arms outstretched and palms turned upward. Position two other people a few yards behind the person with outstretched arms, you can take a picture in which the near person appears to be holding the two other people in his or her hands (Fig. 4-12).

Figure 4-12

Camera

A picture of someone apparently suspended in midair can be taken quite easily. Have a friend stand at one side of a full-length mirror or a reflective store window. Take the photograph at some distance beyond the other side of the mirror or window as shown in Fig. 4-13. Have the subject to be photographed raise the leg exposed to the camera while his other leg and half his body is hidden from view by the mirror. The visible half of your friend's body, together with the image of that visible half, will produce a photograph of a person who appears to be suspended in space.

Figure 4-13

Simply turning a photograph 90 degrees can sometimes produce the illusion of someone doing something impossible. For example, a photograph of someone leaning forward as she walks along a horizontal wall will, when turned 90 degrees, show the same person ascending a vertical wall.

How many more trick photographs can you design and take?

After you have assembled a few such photographs, you can arrange them in an attractive exhibit. Print placed near your photos might read:

Can you guess how each of these photographs was taken?

Mystery shadows

Photographs of shadows are particularly interesting to people. This exhibit reveals how shadow pictures might be used as exhibits at your museum.

Materials

> camera
> film
> 4 or 5 sheets of stiff cardboard, appx. 16 × 32 inches
> colorful cloth to cover cardboard
> transparent packing tape
> scissors
> quick-drying glue

Take photographs of shadows together with the objects that cast them. Develop two prints of each negative. Crop one of the photographs in each pair so that only the shadow is seen.

Photos might include shadows of animals—a dog, horse, cow, giraffe, and so on or shadows cast by players in various sports, such as baseball (the shadow of a pitcher in mid-windup or a batter awaiting a pitch), football (a punter or passer in action), basketball (a player shooting or dunking a basketball), lacrosse (lacrosse sticks make interesting shadows), tennis (a player in the process of making a serve), and so on.

Objects photographed up close with no background clues to their identity can also cast interesting shadows. Ornate, wire, or picket fences, tennis nets, metal staircases, such as fire escapes or those on large water tanks, bridges, icicles, machines, and other objects might be difficult for visitors to guess.

When your collection of photographs has grown large enough to make an interesting exhibit, measure enough material to cover one side of each piece of cardboard to make an attractive backdrop for your display (the actual number of displays you'll need depends on the number of photographs you've taken). Tape the cloth on the back side. If the tape will not hold the cloth, use a stapler or glue as a reinforcement. Arrange the shadow photographs on the cloth-covered side and glue in place, then challenge visitors to guess what it was that cast the shadow:

What animals cast these shadows?

In what sport was each of these shadows cast?

Can you identify the objects that cast each of these shadows?

Shadows and time

This exhibit, which shows the *effects of the season* on shadow length, is interesting but takes one year to prepare.

Materials

➤ camera
➤ film
➤ post or vertical stick driven into level ground
➤ pen and paper

Take four photographs of a post and its shadow at midday in late June, September, December, and March. Of course, the pictures taken in September and March will have shadows that are equal or nearly equal in length. Both dates are near an equinox, which is when the sun is directly above the equator. Near an equinox, the sun's path across the sky will be very much the same. An additional clue, such as a patch of snow, fallen leaves, or a lawn mower, might be included in the photographs to help viewers identify the correct month.

A question posted near these photographs might read:

These photographs were all taken at noon. At what time of the year was each photograph taken? (Answers will vary, but viewers should certainly be able to distinguish the wintertime photo from the one taken in the summer.)

As a sequel to this exhibit, you can take photographs of the same post or vertical stick and its shadow at approximately three-hour intervals so that you have photos at about 6:00 A.M., 9:00 A.M., 12:00 P.M., 3:00 P.M., and 6:00 P.M. Exhibit the photographs in the sequence in which they were taken. The information accompanying these photos might read:

These photographs of a post were taken at different times during a single day. Estimate the time at which each photo was taken. Using the photographs of the post's shadow, imagine that you are standing next to the post. How would you turn to face North? South? East? West? (Answers will vary, but people living above latitude 23.5 degrees North should be able to suggest that the middle shadow is the one that points in a northerly direction if not due North.)

Mystery photos

This exhibit is simple and fun to put together and your patrons will love the puzzle of it. The idea is to see if visitors can identify photographs of objects.

Materials

➤ camera
➤ film
➤ 4 or 5 sheets of stiff cardboard, appx. 16 × 32 inches
➤ colorful cloth to cover cardboard
➤ transparent packing tape
➤ scissors
➤ straight pins
➤ stapler and staples

Take photographs of objects that you think people will have difficulty identifying. For example, a photograph of the filter in an air conditioner or furnace, an upward directed photo of an open steel tower, or a time exposure with the camera pointed at the North Star are all possibilities. You can probably think of many other photos that might serve as excellent mystery photographs. Additional possibilities include pictures taken through a telescope, a microscope, or even an electron microscope. You may be able to find such pictures in old books or magazines.

When your collection of photographs has grown large enough to make an interesting exhibit, measure enough material to cover one side of each piece of cardboard to make an attractive backdrop for your display (the actual number of displays you'll need depends on the number of photographs you've taken). Tape the cloth on the back side. If the tape will not hold the cloth, use a stapler as a reinforcement. Arrange the mystery photographs on the cloth-covered side and pin or tape in place, then challenge visitors to identify the objects:

Can you identify the objects in these pictures?

After a few days, you could print the answers and place them in the exhibit.

Water's skin

This exhibit demonstrates the cohesiveness of water. Visitors will enjoy seeing how cohesiveness can almost appear to be magic.

Materials

➢ dinner fork
➢ paper clip
➢ glass full of water

Fill a glass with clean water. Using the fork, very gently place the paper clip on the surface of the water. If you have difficulty doing this, it might be because the water or the glass is contaminated. Even small amounts of soap residue reduce the water's surface tension enough to prevent it from supporting the paper clip. If this is the case, continue to rinse the glass or, if necessary, find a different glass or container.

The information accompanying this exhibit might be similar to the following:

Water molecules are very cohesive, that is they are strongly attracted to one another. In fact, the molecules on the surface of water are pulled so strongly inward by the molecules beneath them that the water acts as if it had a skin.

Normally, a paper clip would sink in water. But if it is gently placed on the surface of the water it will not break through the water's "skin." The paper clip seen here was placed on the water in this way. If you look closely, you can see the indentations the paper clip makes in the water's skin.

If even a single drop of soapy water were added to the beaker, the water would lose its cohesiveness and the paper clip would break through the surface. You can see this for yourself by preparing this exhibit in your own kitchen and then adding a drop of soapy water.

This exhibit should be enclosed where visitors cannot touch it, such as behind glass. Very little force is required to push the paper clip through the surface.

Eggs that sink; eggs that float

One egg floats in the middle of the liquid in one jar, while the other egg rests on the bottom of the second jar. Visitors will be curious about why one egg floats and the other egg doesn't.

Materials

➢ 2 eggs
➢ 2 tall glass jars
➢ water
➢ table salt
➢ liquid measuring cup
➢ teaspoon

Place one of the eggs in one of the jars, then fill the jar approximately half way up with water. The egg will remain on the bottom of the jar. Place the other egg in the other jar and fill it half way up with water. Dissolve as much salt as you can in 1 cup of water. Tilt one of the jars and slowly pour the salt solution down the inside wall of the jar. Because the saltwater is more dense than the plain water, most of it will come to rest on the bottom of the jar.

The jar containing the salt solution will cause the egg to float. The egg should come to rest on the boundary between the saltwater and the fresh water.

Place the jars on the table with the following question:

These two eggs are identical. Why do you think one egg floats in the middle of the liquid and the other rests on the bottom of the jar?" (Answer: Because inside the jar where the egg floats, the bottom of the jar contains saltwater, which is more dense than an egg, but an egg is more dense than fresh water, which floats on the saltwater.)

This exhibit could be presented with the "Liquid layers" exhibit in Part 5.

Other ideas for exhibits

➤ Photographs of the tracks left by various vehicles—car, truck, tractor, sled, bicycle, tricycle, snowmobile, skis, snowshoes, sled, etc. might make a good puzzle to ponder. The question, "What made each of these tracks?" would be the only print needed in the exhibit.

➤ Interesting shadow patterns can be found and photographed beneath leafy trees on bright sunny days. Sunlight coming through the tiny openings between the leaves produce pinhole images of the sun, or *sun dapples* (see "Pinhole images" in Part 2).

➤ Invite visitors to use a magic wand to demonstrate the persistence of vision. When a white stick is moved rapidly up and down in front of a slide projector, the entire projected image can be seen on the moving stick.

➤ Prepare a display of moiré patterns.

Part 5

Eyes-on exhibits

The exhibits described in Part 5 contain living and nonliving materials that undergo change. They are "eyes-on" rather than hands-on exhibits and are most appropriate in a museum setting where people can and do return on a regular basis.

Depending on the display, you should encourage visitors to revisit these exhibits hourly, daily, weekly, or monthly to observe the changes and patterns that evolve. For example, visitors can see germinating seeds change from one day to the next. The same is true of fast-growing plants. Patrons can best view on an hourly basis exhibits such as the mapping of the sun's path across the sky or the changes on a sundial. On the other hand, the shifting of the sun's position at midday (analemma) is a pattern that evolves slowly and is best viewed on a weekly or monthly schedule. Alert your patrons to the most appropriate viewing routine to follow.

Germinating seeds

There is something almost magical about a germinating seed. With the addition of moisture and warmth, a dormant object begins to change and gives rise to a young growing plant. In this exhibit, viewers will be able to watch seeds as they germinate and produce new plants.

Materials

➤ corn, bean, and pea seeds, dozen each
➤ shallow aluminum or plastic tray, appx. 1 square foot
➤ paper towels
➤ clear plastic wrap
➤ self-adhesive labels
➤ table

Line the tray with layers of damp (not wet) paper towels. Place approximately a dozen seeds of each type on the towels. Cover the seeds and towels with clear plastic wrap to prevent them from drying out. Leave one end of the plastic loose so air can reach the seeds. The clear wrap allows people to see the seeds while reducing moisture loss due to evaporation.

Stick labels on the plastic wrap identifying the seeds. The following printed questions can be placed near the seeds.

Will seeds germinate without soil? If you think they will, which seeds do you think will germinate first?

Then add a statement such as:

Come back each day to see if your predictions were correct.

Once the seeds have germinated, you might add a new question:

What is different about these germinating seeds?

To encourage your museum patrons to conduct their own experiments, you might prepare questions that ask:

Will birdseed germinate? How can you find out?

Planting seeds

This exhibit enables visitors to observe experiments that investigate the effects of planting depth and seed orientation on seed germination and growth. It will also encourage them to carry out a number of related experiments.

Materials

➤ small stones or marbles, enough to fill 1 inch of a 10-gallon aquarium or 2 wide-mouth jars

➤ 10-gallon glass aquarium or 2 wide-mouth jars

➤ 5-pound bag of potting soil or topsoil

➤ ruler

➤ 15 corn seeds

➤ clear plastic wrap

➤ sand or gravel, enough to fill 1 inch of a 10-gallon aquarium or 2 wide-mouth jars

➤ tabletop

Place approximately 1 inch of small stones or marbles on the bottom of the aquarium or jars. Add approximately 1 inch of sand or gravel on top of this. The stones and gravel or sand allow water to drain from the soil and keep the seeds from rotting. Finally, pour approximately 8 inches of potting soil or topsoil into the aquarium or jars.

Place approximately five corn seeds on the surface of the soil. Plant another five corn seeds at each of the following depths: 1 inch, 2 inches, 4 inches, and 6 inches. Orient the seeds in different ways (Fig. 5-1). Be sure the seeds are visible through the glass so people can see them. The soil should be kept moist but not wet.

Figure 5-1

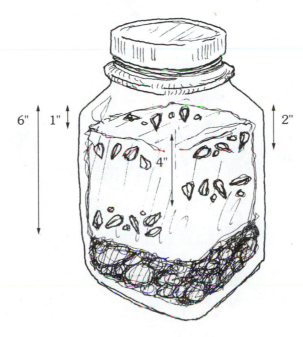

The following question, or a similar one, should appear near the exhibit:

How does the depth that seeds are planted affect their germination and growth?

Once the seeds begin to germinate, you can add more questions.

Does the depth that the seeds are planted affect the time it takes them to germinate? (Answer: No, but if planted too deep in the soil, they will not emerge from the soil before the food stored in the seed is depleted.)

What happens if the seeds are upside down? Do the roots still grow down and the stems grow up? (Answer: Yes, roots grow down; stems and leaves grow up.)

To encourage visitors to conduct their own experiments, you might add such questions as:

How do you think temperature will affect the germination of seeds? Do you think pea seeds will germinate in colder temperatures than corn seeds?

Do you think seeds will germinate faster in one type of soil than in another?

Do you think young plants will grow better in one type of soil than in another?

Finally, you could suggest:

Design and carry out experiments of your own to answer these questions.

The life cycle of a plant

In this ongoing exhibit, you will provide viewers with an opportunity to watch the life cycle of a pea plant. They will see the germinated seeds grow, flower, produce fruit (pods), and finally form seeds in the pods.

Materials

➢ sunny area
➢ 2 flowerpots or a window box
➢ 5-pound bag of potting soil
➢ ruler
➢ 12 pea seeds
➢ 12 sticks, appx. 3 feet long
➢ optional: thin plastic bag and heavy wire or 4 thin sticks

Plant the seeds approximately 1 inch beneath the soil. Plant two or three seeds per pot or approximately 2 inches apart in a window box. Peas are normally planted in the early spring and require 60 to 70 days to complete their life cycle. Pea plants also need a sunny area.

Keep the soil damp but not wet. If the plants are grown indoors and the air in the room is very dry, you can build your own greenhouse by placing a large, thin plastic bag over the container as a cover for the plants. The plastic retards the loss of water but allows the exchange of gases between the plants and the atmosphere. To keep the plastic off the plants, you might need to build a small frame with sticks or heavy wire. You will also need long, upright sticks to support the pea stems as they grow.

Pea plants do not thrive in hot weather; consequently, don't try to grow them in a hot room. A cool or moderately warm area provides the best environment for good growth.

Some statements and questions that might accompany this exhibit are the following:

Seeds are planted in this soil. Watch the soil and look for plants to emerge, then return frequently to watch the plants grow, blossom, bear fruit, and produce seeds. Can you identify the plants that are growing here? (Answer: They are pea plants.) Where are the seeds of this plant? (Answer: In the pod.)

Growing grass on a turntable

This exhibit reveals how forces affect the growth of a plant, in this case, grass, rye, or corn. Growing seedlings on a spinning table subjects them to a centrifugal force. The seedlings "feel" a force that seems to be pushing them outward.

Materials

> thick cardboard, appx. 16 × 32 inches
> turntable
> pie pan or long plastic dish (as long as the diameter of the turntable)
> potting soil, enough to fill pan or dish
> grass, rye, or corn seeds
> tabletop
> heavy-duty scissors
> access to an electrical outlet
> well lighted location

Cut a piece of the cardboard to cover the surface of an old turntable. Nearly fill the pie pan or plastic dish with moist potting soil. Spread grass or rye seeds on the soil, then sprinkle a very thin layer of soil over the seeds. If you wish, you can use corn seeds in place of grass or rye seeds but you will have to push the corn seeds approximately 1 inch or so into the dirt.

Place the pan or dish on the turntable in a well lighted location. Plug the cord from the turntable into an electrical outlet so that it turns and the seeds "feel" a centrifugal force as they germinate (Fig. 5-2). Add water to the soil occasionally to keep it damp but not wet.

Figure

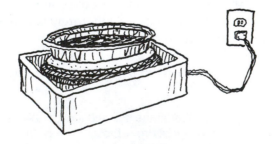

Once the plants have germinated and can be seen moving around and around on the turntable, place information such as the following near the spinning plants:

On a merry-go-round, you feel as if there is a force pushing you outward. This force is called *centrifugal force* and can be felt whenever you move along a curved path, be it on a merry-go-round, a playground whirl-around, a loop-the-loop roller coaster, or a bicycle rounding a corner. The force feels just as real as gravity. In order to maintain your balance, you compensate by leaning inward toward the center of the circular path you are following. You have probably done this many times on your bicycle.

Look at the plants spinning on the turntable. Which way did the plants grow? What evidence is there that plants respond to centrifugal force? What evidence is there that the centrifugal force grows larger as the distance from the center of the turntable increases? (Answers: The plants grow inward, opposite to the direction of the force. This is similar to the way they grow upward, opposite to the direction of the force of gravity. The combination of the two forces causes the slanted inward growth. The further the plants are from the center of the turntable, the more they bend.

Does the speed of rotation affect the plant's growth pattern? Does it matter whether the rotation begins before or after the seeds have germinated? (Answer: Yes, the faster the rotation, the more the plants lean inward.

A mold garden

In this ongoing exhibit, which can remain in place for a year or more, museum visitors will have the opportunity to see a variety of molds and witness their capacity to decompose materials.

Materials

> ➤ 10-gallon aquarium, clear plastic container, or large glass jar
> ➤ sand, enough to fill container 1 inch
> ➤ various items to put in the the sand (see text)
> ➤ thin plastic bag or clear plastic wrap
> ➤ tabletop
> ➤ ruler

Spread approximately 1 inch of moist sand over the bottom of the container, aquarium, or jar. Put a number of different materials onto the sand. You might include pieces of bread, fruit, vegetables, leather, wood, paper, plastic, metal, rock, glass, and a variety of cloths such as cotton, nylon, silk, wool, and so on. Cover the jar with the plastic bag or wrap so that the sand remains moist.

Place information such as the following near the mold garden:

Molds are non-green plants that serve as one of the major agents of decay. You have probably seen a piece of moldy bread or the mildew that grows on damp wood, cloth, or leather. Some molds are beautiful; others are yucky. But all molds, unlike green plants, are unable to manufacture their own food by photosynthesis. Some molds are green, but the green is not the chlorophyll used by plants to produce food from sunlight, carbon dioxide, and water. Molds obtain their food from living or dead plants and animals or one or more of the many products of living things. Molds reproduce by producing spores. The spores are tiny and abundant and can be found on almost everything. On which object in this mold garden do you think mold will first appear? (Answers vary.)

Later you might ask:

How many different types of mold can you see in this mold garden? Which mold seems to be the most common? (Answers vary.) On which objects does mold not seem to grow? (Answer: Materials such as rocks, metal, glass, ceramics, and chalk, to name a few.) Which objects do not seem to decay despite all the mold in the garden? (Answer: Materials on which mold does not grow; the molds cannot decompose these nonorganic materials.)

After about a year, you will probably want to discard the exhibit. Put it in a heavy bag before disposal.

Bird watching

Many people enjoy watching and identifying birds. This exhibit will give your museum visitors the opportunity to do both.

Materials

> ➢ birdseed
> ➢ box of raisins
> ➢ suet
> ➢ cheese
> ➢ cardboard, appx. 16 × 32 inches
> ➢ window to the outdoors
> ➢ plastic or aluminum tray, appx. 16 × 32 inches
> ➢ large pan or trash can cover
> ➢ water
> ➢ bird feeder[1]
> ➢ photographs or illustrations of birds found in your area

Your museum must have a window to the outside so birds can be observed. You can build simple feeders to attract birds to your museum's observation post (your window) or you can set food on the ground in trays if there are no squirrels or cats nearby.

Seeds and raisins will attract chickadees, sparrows, and cardinals. Cheese and suet (can be found in many meat markets) will attract woodpeckers and nuthatches.

Fill the trays or feeders (Fig. 5-3) with the cheese, suet, raisins, or birdseed, depending on what type of birds you are trying to attract. If

Figure 5-3

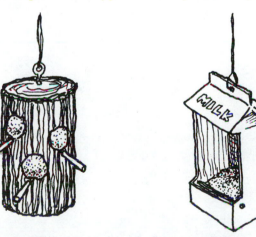

1 Some birds prefer hanging feeders, which you can make from empty milk cartons or logs (Fig. 5-3). The cartons can be cut on their sides and filled with birdseed and hung with twine. The log feeders can have holes drilled in their sides and then filled with suet, cheese, or peanut butter and hung with stiff wire. Have an adult help you build a hanging feeder.

you want visitors to figure out what type of food attracts what birds, fill different feeders with different food. Fill the trash can lid or large pan with water to serve as a birdbath. If the water freezes, break it away and add fresh water.

On a table or easel near the observation window, display the photographs and illustrations of the birds commonly found in your area. To accompany the pictures you might add some questions such as:

How many of these birds have you seen at the feeders outside this window? Have you seen any that are not shown here? (Answers will vary.)

The shifting sun:
A hallway sundial

In this exhibit visitors will use a simple sun clock, or gnomon, to indicate time. They will discover that sun time and clock time do not always agree.

This exhibit and the next two exhibits could be set up side by side.

Materials

- south-facing window
- 2 pencils
- modeling clay
- 4 sheets of 8½ × 11 white paper
- clock
- transparent tape
- table
- twine
- thin board, appx. 8½ × 11
- saw
- thick board to use as a base for the thin board, appx. 1 foot square
- wood glue
- 2 C-clamps
- white paint
- paintbrush
- dark-colored marker
- protractor

Tape the four sheets of paper together so that you have a large square. Place the table beneath a south-facing window, and tape the paper onto the tabletop. Place a small lump of clay on the middle of the end of the paper near the window and stick the pencil (gnomon) into it. Put the clock on the table or on a wall nearby.

Draw a line along the pencil's shadow at one-hour intervals during the course of a sunny day. Record the time on the paper next to each hour line you draw (Fig. 5-4).

You might also like to record the position of the shadow at midday—the time when the sun reaches maximum altitude and is due South. Midday actually depends on where you live. It cannot be found with a clock because noon is not necessarily midday according to the sun. The sun reaches its peak point in the sky at the eastern end of a time zone before it reaches the same point at locations farther west.

Figure 5-4

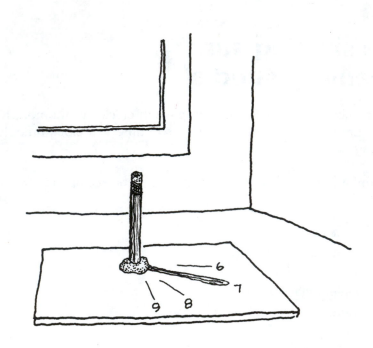

Here is a way to mark midday and find the direction of true North for points north of the Tropic of Cancer (latitude = 23.5° N). At about 11:00 A.M. (standard time), use a string and a pencil to make a semicircle around the gnomon whose shadow is serving as a clock hand. The radius of the semicircle should be the length of the gnomon's shadow at 11:00 A.M. As midday approaches, the gnomon's shadow grows shorter; after midday it grows longer. Mark the spot where the shadow again touches the semicircle. Draw a straight line connecting the mark and the point where the 11:00 A.M. line touches the semicircle. A line from the upright gnomon to the center of the line you have just drawn points due North. The same line indicates the direction of the gnomon's shadow at midday. By sunset, you will have a series of hour lines as well as a line that marks midday and the direction of north.

The information and questions that accompany this exhibit might read as follows:

These lines mark the position of the pencil's shadow at the hours indicated on (give date lines were made). The line drawn from the pencil to the midpoint of the line connecting points on a semicircle points due North and marks the point of midday on (give date lines were made). Test this shadow clock's accuracy with the clock each day throughout the year. Is the shadow clock an accurate timepiece throughout the year? (Answer: No it is not accurate throughout the year because the stick is not parallel to the earth's axis. As a result, the stick's shadow is not always in agreement with the hands of a clock.)

Although a shadow clock does not keep accurate time throughout the year, the exhibit does reveal why sundials are not made with a vertical stick. A more accurate sundial—one with a slanting gnomon—can be built to replace the simple shadow clock.

The gnomon must be cut at an angle so that it is parallel to the earth's axis. For example, if you live at a latitude of 40 degrees, the gnomon should slant upward 40 degrees from the horizontal.

Ask an adult to help you cut such a gnomon from the thin board (Fig. 5-5). Glue the gnomon to the board that will serve as the base. Use the C-clamps to support the gnomon until the glue dries. When the glue has dried, paint the base white to make the lines you will draw on it more distinct.

Figure 5-5

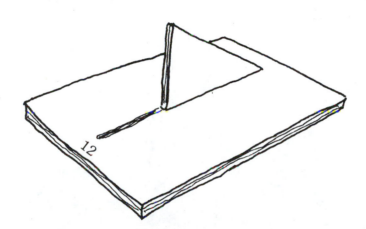

On a sunny day when the shadow of the stick in your first sundial lies on the line that points due North, place the new sundial so that the gnomon's shadow points due North. You will know it points due North if it casts no shadow on either side of the gnomon.

Mark a line through the center of the shadow north of the gnomon and mark it "12." This local solar noon, as recorded on your new sundial, might differ from noon on your clock. The difference depends on your location within your time zone and on the sun, which is sometimes ahead of clock time and sometimes behind it. This will become more evident if you build another exhibit called "An Analemma," which is described later in Part 5.

Exactly one hour after you have marked 12 on the dial, draw a line along the edge of the shadow cast by the sloping edge of the gnomon. Label this line "1." Continue to mark lines in this way at one-hour intervals until sunset. You now have all the lines you need to calibrate a sundial that measures sun time.

To draw lines for the morning hours, simply measure the angles of the afternoon lines with a protractor, then draw the mirror image of the afternoon lines on the morning side of the gnomon.

The information and questions that accompany this new sundial exhibit might read as follows:

This is an improved sundial. The angle that the slanted wooden gnomon makes with the horizon is equal to the latitude of this location (give latitude). As a result, the gnomon's upper edge is parallel to the earth's axis.

The clock near the exhibit was set to 12:00 noon when the sundial indicated midday on (give date dial was set). Midday might not have been 12:00 noon on your watch. In fact, it was (give actual clock time) on our watches when the sundial was set for noon according to the sun. Check this sundial's accuracy with the clock each day throughout the year. Is it a more accurate timepiece than the earlier shadow dial. (Answer: Yes, but it still doesn't always agree with the clock.)

An analemma

As you found in the last exhibit, even an improved sundial does not match clock time throughout the year. This is because a clock measures a mean solar day—the length of an average day. But a mean solar day can differ from an actual solar day. This exhibit will show visitors that a mean solar day of 24 hours, as measured by a clock, differs from the actual sun time.

Materials

➤ south-facing window
➤ thin cardboard, long enough to cover the bottom of a window
➤ transparent tape
➤ ruler
➤ table or countertop
➤ scissors
➤ sheet of 8½ × 11 white paper
➤ pen or pencil
➤ optional: mirror and colored stick pins

Place the thin cardboard over the bottom of a south-facing window and tape it into place. A table or a countertop should be near the bottom of the cardboard. Tape a sheet of white paper to the table or counter. Make a small hole through the cardboard approximately 4 inches (10 centimeters) above the paper. The sun's pinhole image should fall at a point near the center of the paper at exactly 12:00 noon. Mark the center of the image with a pen or pencil and write the date in small numbers beside the mark (Fig. 5-6).

Figure 5-6

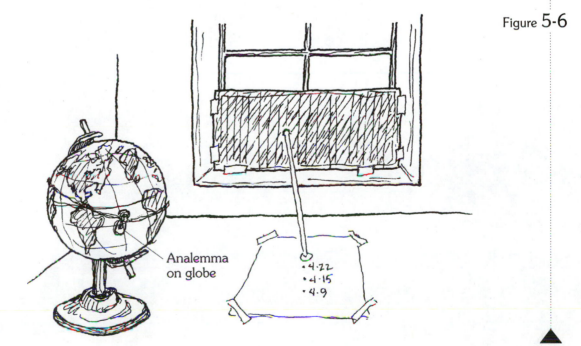

Analemma
on globe

· 4·22
· 4·15
· 4·9

Repeat this procedure at exactly noon as often as possible on sunny days. You need not do it every day. Even if you mark the sun's noon-time position only once a week, a pattern will become evident over the course of a few months.

If the composition of the ceiling near this exhibit is appropriate for marking with colored stick pins, you can use a mirror to reflect the sun's noon-time position on the paper onto the ceiling. This will magnify the analemma's pattern considerably. This exhibit can be further enhanced by placing a globe with its analemma visible near the paper where the pattern is being mapped.

The information provided viewers of this seemingly simple exhibit might include the way it is set up and marked as well as the following:

It is not surprising to see the sun's image, which is marked on the paper at noon, move farther from the window during the winter and closer during the warmer months. After all, the sun rises higher in the sky in the summer than it does in the winter. But the spots, marked at exactly the same time according to the clock, do not lie along a straight North-South line. What does this tell you about the sun's position in the sky at noon? During which weeks of the year does the sun run ahead of the clock? During which weeks of the year is sun time behind clock time? How does your pattern of spots compare with the analemma seen on globes? (Answer: The sun is not always at the same position along a North-South line at noon each day. Sun time runs ahead of clock time from mid-April to mid-June and from September through most of December. It falls behind clock time from late December to mid-April and from mid-June to September. The pattern is similar to the analemma seen on globes. The variation in sun time is caused by the earth's elliptical orbit.)

The seasonal paths of the sun

The sun's path across the sky changes significantly over the course of a year. In this exhibit, you will map the sun's path and then display the results. Both the mapping and the results can provide the basis for this exhibit.

Materials

➤ 3 or 4 transparent plastic domes, appx. 8 inches in diameter
➤ 3 or 4 pieces of heavy cardboard, appx. 16 × 32 inches
➤ colored markers
➤ transparent tape
➤ sunny window or outdoor area
➤ table
➤ clock

Put the clear dome, or "hemisphere," on a sheet of heavy cardboard, and mark the outline of its circular base on the cardboard. Remove the dome and mark a colored dot at the very center of the circle. The dot represents the position of a person looking at the sky, which seems to be shaped like an overhead dome and is known as the *celestial hemisphere*. Put the plastic hemisphere back on the cardboard exactly where it was before and tape it securely in place.

To map the sun's path across the sky—which can be part of the exhibit if viewers can return periodically during a sunny day—put the dome on the cardboard and on a table in front of a sunny window or on a flat area outdoors. As soon as the sun reaches the transparent hemisphere, place the tip of a marking pen on the dome so that its shadow falls on the dot you marked at the center of the circle (Fig. 5-7). Mark this point on the dome. This mark represents the sun's position in the sky because it is directly in line with the dot at the center of the circle and the sun.

Continue marking the dome at hour or half-hour intervals. By sunset, you'll have a map of the sun's path across the sky that you can display.

Repeat the experiment on other sunny days over the course of a year. Try to make these maps of the sun's path at times close to the equinoxes (September 20 and March 20) and the summer and winter solstices (June 20 and December 20).

The exhibit will consist of the growing collection of domes showing the path of the sun across the sky. Label each dome with the date the sun's path was recorded.

Figure 5-7

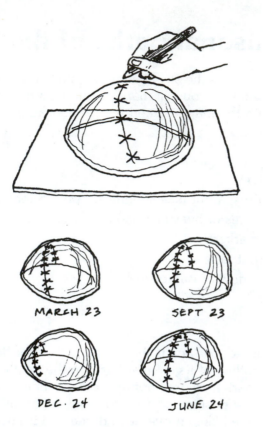

MARCH 23

SEPT 23

DEC. 24

JUNE 24

The information accompanying this exhibit might read as follows:

The clear domes (hemispheres) show the sun's path across the sky at different times of the year. The dots were made at different times of the day with a marker that was in line with the sun and a dot at the center of the dome. What do you think the sun's path across the sky will look like a month from today? Six months from today? A year from today? (Answers: The answers to the first two questions will vary depending on the time of the year. The sun's path a year from today would be the same as it is today.)

Liquid layers

This exhibit, which is about density and solubility, reveals that a less dense substance will float on a more dense one. However, once mixed, liquids will separate only if they are not soluble in one another.

Materials

- 4 test tubes
- stand for test tubes
- 3 or 4 small stones
- water
- few wood shavings
- 1-pound bag of kosher salt
- 2 measuring cups, one for liquids
- food coloring
- container for mixing salt and water, appx. 2 quarts
- 4, 2-liter soda bottles with screw-on caps
- funnel
- eyedropper
- cooking oil
- marker
- stirring rods

The exhibit consists of four test tubes containing different substances with different densities.

Fill the bottom of the first tube with the small stones, add water, then add some small pieces of wood to float on the top (Fig. 5-8a).

The second tube will be filled with four liquid layers—red, green, clear, and blue (Fig. 5-8b)—made from water and three different salt solutions.

To make the red liquid, add 1 cup of kosher salt to 1 quart of water and stir until the salt is dissolved. (Kosher salt is used to avoid the cloudiness that results when ordinary table salt is used.) Once the salt is dissolved, add red food coloring, a drop at a time, until the liquid is a deep red color. Put the funnel into one of the soda bottles and pour the solution into it.

Make the green liquid by dissolving ⅔ cup of kosher salt in 1 quart of water and add green food coloring, then pour into the second bottle. To make the clear liquid, dissolve ⅓ cup of kosher salt in a quart of water and pour into the third bottle. Make the blue liquid by adding blue food coloring to water and pouring it into the fourth bottle. Seal the bottles of liquid and store them. Each day you will have to prepare fresh liquid layers.

Pour a little of the "lightest" (least dense) blue liquid (water) into the bottom of one of the tubes. Use an eyedropper to add the clear liquid, which is the least concentrated salt solution. Place the tip of the liquid-filled eyedropper on the bottom of the tube and slowly squeeze the liquid into the tube. The clear salt solution, being denser than the blue water, will form a layer beneath the water as shown in Fig. 5-8e.

Next, use the eyedropper to layer the green salt solution beneath the clear solution. Finally, the red liquid can be placed at the bottom of the tube by using the eyedropper in the same way.

The third test tube, which has been shaken, contains a mixture of the four liquids (Fig. 5-8c).

The fourth test tube, which could be available as a hands-on display, contains water and a few milliliters of cooking oil (Fig. 5-8d). The oil, which is insoluble in water and also less dense than water, floats on top of the water.

Figure 5-8

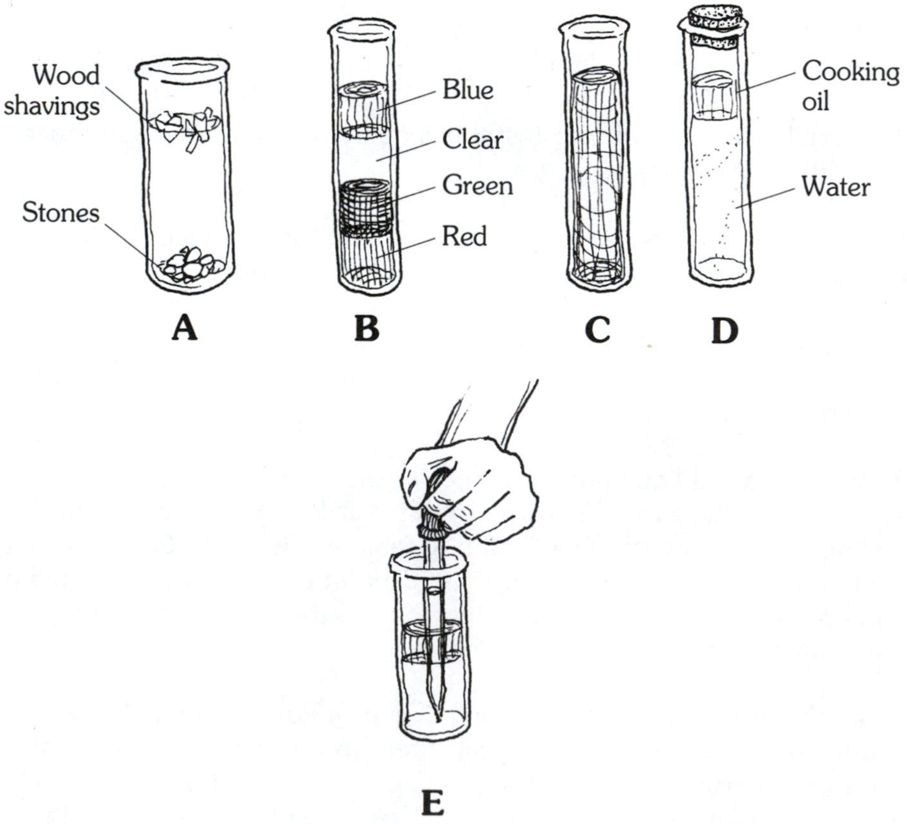

A   B   C   D

E

The information accompanying this small but colorful display might read:

Density is the heaviness of a substance—the weight per volume. The denser the substance the more weight it has for the same volume. For example, seawater, which contains salt, is denser than pure water.

The first tube contains a liquid, some stones, and wood. What can you tell about the densities of these three substances? What might the liquid be? (Answers: The stones are the densest substance; the wood is the least dense; the liquid's density is greater than wood but less than stone. The liquid could be water or any other liquid with a density greater than wood but less than stone.)

The second tube contains four different liquids. What can you say about the densities of these four liquids? Three of the liquids are salt solutions; one is water. Which liquid do you think is water? How do you think the other three solutions were made in order to form separate layers? Do your own experiments to see if you can figure out how the liquids remain separated in distinct layers. (Answers: The liquids have different densities. The blue solution is water; it floats on the others and is, therefore, the least dense of the four. The liquid layers could be made by dissolving different amounts of salt in the same volume of water and then adding a dye or they could be any four liquids with different densities.)

The third tube contains a mixture of all four of the liquids found in the second tube. Why don't the liquids separate to form distinct layers? (Answer: The liquids are all soluble [dissolvable] in one another. Once they mix, the density of the liquid becomes the same throughout.)

The fourth tube contains cooking oil and water. Which liquid is denser? If you shake the tube, will the liquids remain mixed or will they separate? Why? If alcohol and water were layered in a tube and then shaken, would they separate again or remain mixed? (Answers: The liquids will separate after shaking because cooking oil does not dissolve in water. If alcohol and water were shaken they would remain mixed because alcohol is soluble in water.)

Climbing water and surface area

The first part of this exhibit reveals that liquids will climb up narrow tubes, a phenomenon know as *capillarity*. The second part of the exhibit shows that the evaporation of liquids as they climb the narrow spaces between the fibers in paper reduces the height to which the liquid rises. Careful analysis of the experiment also indicates that the rate of evaporation is related to the surface area of the paper that is exposed to the air.

Materials

➤ various glass tubes with differing inside diameters[2]
➤ 11-x-13-inch sheet of white cardboard
➤ stiff cardboard, appx. 5 × 12 inches
➤ transparent or masking tape
➤ food coloring
➤ blotter paper or paper towels[3]
➤ 2 shallow pie or cake pans
➤ ruler
➤ scissors
➤ magnifying lens
➤ brick or table set against a wall
➤ scissors
➤ 2 C-clamps and 2 ring stands or a cabinet
➤ optional: polyethylene tubing, plastic wrap, or wax paper

To demonstrate capillarity, pour water into the shallow pan and add food coloring. Tape the various glass or plastic tubes to the white cardboard so that their ends extend beyond the cardboard as shown in Fig. 5-9a. Write each tube's inside diameter above the tube on the cardboard. Lean the cardboard up against a wall or prop it up with a brick and put the ends of the tubes into the pan of colored water. The colored water makes it possible to see the level of the water in each of the tubes where capillarity is evident.

The information accompanying the exhibit might be similar to the following:

Water rises above its normal level when it is in contact with narrow openings. The attraction between water and glass pulls water up the tubes. The effect is known as *capillarity*. The inside diameters of these tubes differ. The actual

---

2 Capillary tubes are best if they are available.

3 Paper towels can be used in place of blotter paper but they are not as sturdy and are more likely to be moved by air currents.

inside diameter of each tube is written above it. How is the height to which the water rises in a tube related to the diameter of the tube? (Answer: the narrower the tube, the higher the water rises.)

The second part of the exhibit demonstrates capillarity using blotter paper strips or paper towels of different widths.

Measure and cut out various strips of paper towels or blotter paper. Each strip should be 12 or more inches long. The width of the strips should vary from approximately ⅛ inch to 2 inches. Strips of ⅛, ¼, ½, 1, 1½, and 2 inches arranged in order of increasing width make an attractive exhibit, as shown in Fig. 5-9b.

Figure 5-9

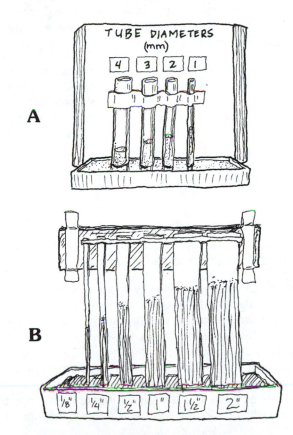

Tape the upper ends of the paper strips to the narrow strip of cardboard, which can then be taped to a cabinet or held in position by clamps attached to ring stands. Write the width of each strip on a self-adhesive label and place it below the strip.

Fill the shallow pan with water and add food coloring. Immerse the lower ends of the strips in the colored water at about the time people begin to visit the exhibit. This way, visitors can return to the exhibit periodically to see how the experiment is progressing. If the air is dry, you might have to add water to the pan to be sure that the ends of the strips remain in contact with the water.

Put the magnifying lens on the table close to the exhibit. The lens will enable viewers to see the tiny fibers that form the structure of blotter paper.

The information and questions placed near the exhibit might read as follows:

Look through the magnifying glass to see the structure of the blotter paper (or the paper towels). The paper consists of tiny fibers. The spaces between the fibers form narrow openings. Water is attracted to the surface of these fibers just as it is attracted to glass. Consequently, water exhibits capillarity with blotter paper (or paper towels) as well as glass. In fact, it is capillarity that enables paper towels to absorb water.

The long vertical strips of blotter paper have their lower ends immersed in colored water to make it possible to see how high the water rises in the strips. The strips are of different widths as indicated by the labels. How high do you think the water will rise in the narrow spaces between the fibers that make up blotter paper? Do you think the width of the strip will have any effect on the height to which the water rises? (Answers will vary.)

Come back as often as you can during the next 24 to 48 hours to see what happens.

After about a day, the water will stop rising. The results will be approximately as shown in Fig. 5-9b. After another day, you might add the following information to the exhibit.

The water has now stopped rising in the tiny spaces between the blotter paper fibers. Did the width of the strip have an effect on the height to which the water rose? Can you explain why? What do you think would happen if we repeated the experiment with the strips covered with plastic so water cannot evaporate from them? (Answers: The water rose higher in the wider strips. Explanations and predictions will vary, but some may suggest that evaporation prevented the water from rising higher. In fact, the water rises until the water losses due to evaporation equal the advances caused by capillarity. If the strips of blotter paper were covered with plastic, the water would rise to the tops of the strips.)

You can continue the exhibit and take the demonstration through one more step. To show what happens when the strips are covered, repeat the experiment with the strips covered with plastic or waxed paper. You can use polyethylene tubing or make your own tubing from plastic wrap or waxed paper sealed with tape. The tops of the tubes should be sealed; the bottoms should be open and in contact with the water. This way, the entire length of the blotter strip is shielded from air but water can still rise in the spaces between the fibers.

Under these conditions, water "climbs" much higher if evaporation is eliminated. Visitors who return to the exhibit will notice that the water rises to the top of the strips when they are covered. You might conclude this ongoing exhibit with the following information placed near the covered strips:

Water rises to the top of these strips when they are covered because water cannot evaporate from the paper. This tells us that the spaces between the fibers in the paper must be very small. How can we explain the earlier experiment in which the water rose higher in the wider strips than in the narrower strips? The answer lies in the fact that the narrower the strip, the greater the surface area per volume of water. Consider a strip that is cut in half. The volume of water in each strip is halved but a new surface where evaporation can take place is formed along the path of the scissors.

Other ideas for exhibits

➢ Set up an aquarium with various interesting fish and plants. You might also develop a sea life aquarium using saltwater.

➢ Set up a terrarium and occasionally change the soil, plants, and animals. For example, you might establish a desertlike climate for one exhibit and a rain forest climate for another.

➢ Collect and grow a variety of weeds. Usually, any soil that you collect will have a variety of weed seeds within it. All you have to do is supply water. Weeds are hardy stock.

Part 6

Exhibits to see

An exhibit might explain a scientific principle very clearly, but if people aren't drawn to it by its appearance, they will never appreciate or learn from its solid content. Consequently, some of the exhibits in Part 6 require an artistic flair, and photographs of trees, tracks, clouds, and flowers can also serve as a source of questions and information as well as beauty. For other exhibits, visitors will be asked to make careful observations, although they will not be actively involved in manipulating materials.

Many exhibits are best displayed as things to see rather than touch. Their shape, color, structure or other features make them interesting and attractive to your museum patrons. These types of displays require a suitable background, such as colored cloth or paper. You might even want to create your own diorama, a scenic painting with sculptured figures and lifelike details. Displays could be surrounded or partially surrounded with glass, plastic, wood, or cardboard.

Print material of a suitable size, style, and color will be essential. Identifying labels should be attractive and neat if a display includes several items.

No matter what the exhibit, you'll want to use your creative talents for the projects in Part 6. Your imagination and creativity will spark enjoyment and interest for your museum visitors as well as give you the satisfaction of a job well done.

Animal tracks

Although stuffed animals make attractive exhibits, their preparation requires extensive training and is best left to experienced professionals. However, animal parts such as bones, teeth, skulls, nests, feathers, eggs, horns, shells, and tracks make interesting collections and can make for exciting exhibits.

This exhibit challenges visitors to identify the animal tracks you've prepared. They can compare the tracks against illustrations you've made or photographs and illustrations you've provided from magazines or field guides. You could also use the electric quiz board described in Part 2 to provide the answers.

Materials

➢ plaster of paris
➢ 4 or 5 stiff paper strips, appx. 3 × 24 inches long
➢ paper clips or transparent tape
➢ table knife
➢ old container to mix the plaster of paris
➢ spoon or paint stirrer
➢ 2 measuring cups, one liquid
➢ 4 or 5 brightly colored ribbons
➢ black or brown acrylic paint
➢ paintbrush
➢ ruler
➢ magazines with photographs and illustrations of animals or field guide[1]
➢ scissors
➢ transparent tape
➢ 5 or 6 lengths of colored ribbon or yarn

In order to make this exhibit interesting, you need to locate four or five different animal tracks. The best areas to locate animal tracks are in locations were there is little human contact, but never venture into secluded areas such as woods without an adult. When you and your parent or other adult find an animal track, mark the location by tying a ribbon or piece of yarn on a nearby bush or tree. You can then go back later that day or the next with the materials you'll need to make casts of the tracks.

If the locations of the tracks are far apart, you might have to make up the plaster of paris at each location because it will begin to

---

1 You can take your own photographs if you're inclined or if you are artistic, create your own illustrations.

harden before you can make a cast of all the tracks. If all the tracks are located in one area, you should be able to make up all of the plaster of paris you'll need at one time.

To make a cast of a track (usually in soft dirt), place one of the heavy strips of paper around the track. Use the paper clips or tape to hold the paper ring in place (Fig. 6-1). Mix up the plaster of paris by following the directions on the carton. Stir the mixture with an old spoon or paint stirrer. Try to make the plaster of paris thick and creamy so that it will pour slowly. To avoid the formation of bubbles in the cast, tap the container on the ground several times to release any air that might be trapped in the mixture before pouring the plaster.

Figure 6-1

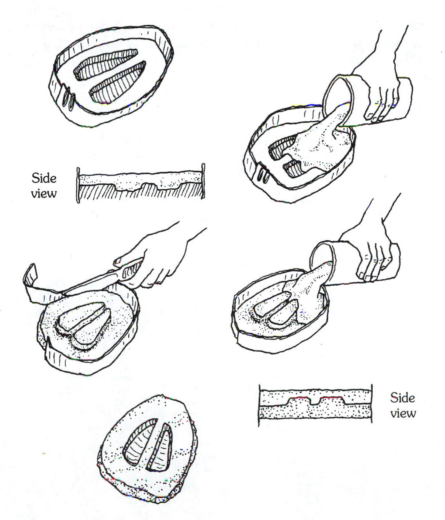

Side view

Side view

Pour the plaster into the track until it completely fills the track. After about 20 minutes, the plaster should be hard. You can then use the table knife to dig around the plaster-filled track and remove it from the ground. Turn it over, wash off the dirt, and, to coin a term from photography, you will have a negative print (cast) of the track.

You can make positive casts of these tracks back at your "workshop." Simply repeat the process, but this time place the heavy paper firmly against the negative cast before pouring plaster of paris over it. To prepare the positive casts for your exhibit, it is a good idea to paint the track depressions with a dark paint. This will make the tracks stand out against the white plaster.

If you have any doubt as to the animal that made the tracks you have cast, you can compare the cast with photographs or drawings of known tracks in a field guide.

Once you've identified the animal tracks, go through the magazines and field guides you've collected and clip out illustrations and photographs of the animal tracks you collected. Look through the encyclopedia and other books on each animal track you collected and type or word process some of the information for your display. Place all of the tracks, information, and illustrations on a table along with a ruler.

Some of the questions you might ask visitors include the following:

Can you guess what type of animal made these tracks? Use the ruler provided and measure the track. Was the animal larger or smaller than you? (Answer will vary depending on the tracks and the measurements.)

Have you seen any of these animals near your home? (Answer will probably be yes if the tracks were collected near the museum.)

Bird nests

This exhibit should be done in the autumn after birds have begun to migrate south. This way, you can be certain that the nests do not contain eggs or baby birds.

Materials

➤ several bird nests
➤ self-adhesive labels
➤ encyclopedia
➤ field guides or other books on birds
➤ photographs or illustrations of birds

Collect several bird nests. The more bird nests you find, the more interesting your exhibit will be. Try to identify the species that made the nests. Some common nests are shown in Fig. 6-2.

Remove some of the materials from each nest and try to identify them. Did the bird(s) use twigs? Grass? Shredded tree bark? Moss? Hair? Mud? Feathers? Label each material for your exhibit and place it next to the nest it came from.

Figure 6-2

Robin

Red-winged
blackbird
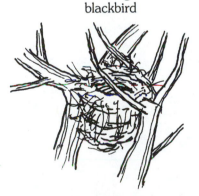

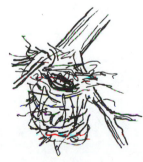
Baltimore
oriole

Sparrow

Look through the encyclopedia and various bird books and learn all you can about bird nests and the type of birds that might have built the nests you've collected. Once you've studied the subject, put all of the information together for your exhibit visitors.

You might then ask the following questions:

Can you identify the birds that made each of these nests? What materials were used to make each nest? (Answers will vary.)

Insect collection

You can learn much about insects by collecting them and preparing an exhibit that museum visitors can enjoy. Collect insects several times from early spring until late fall. You will find more insects in the summer, but it is interesting to see how the types of insects you collect varies from month to month.

Materials

➤ 2 or 3, 1-gallon clear plastic food storage bag
➤ insect net[2]
➤ wire twist tie or rubber band
➤ white bed sheet
➤ 4 or 5 jars with lids
➤ 10-gallon aquarium
➤ screen to cover aquarium
➤ entomology books
➤ heavy-duty scissors
➤ cardboard to use as displays
➤ push pins
➤ glue
➤ wooden or heavy cardboard box for displaying dead insects
➤ corrugated cardboard
➤ 2 or 3 sheets of 8½ × 11 paper or construction paper
➤ 3-x-5-inch file cards
➤ optional: colorful cloth or paper to cover box or corrugated cardboard

This exhibit is divided into two parts. The first part explains how to capture and display live insects. The second part of the exhibit is more permanent—it is a collection of dead insects.

For a live exhibit, you must first capture living insects. One way to capture live insects is to walk through an open field swinging an insect net back and forth in front of you as you walk. Once you have captured some insects, keep the net sealed while someone covers it with the clear plastic bag. Remove your hand just before your partner seals the mouth of the bag around the net's handle with a twist-tie or a rubber band. Turn the net inside out within the plastic bag.

---

2 You can purchase an insect net or make one. Shape one end of a wire coat hanger into a circle and leave the other end in a straight extension. Fasten a cheesecloth bag to the coat hanger, and secure the extension to an old mop handle or dowel with heavy-duty tape (Fig. 6-3).

Figure 6-3

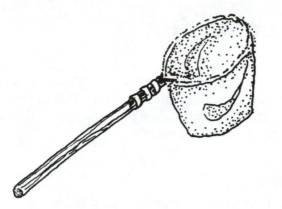

Another way to collect insects is to put a white sheet under a small tree or bush. Shake the bush, and a variety of insects will fall onto the sheet where they are easy to see and capture. If you want some nocturnal insects for your collection, simply turn on an outdoor light at dark and use your net to capture them.

You can also search for insects in grass, flowers, old leaves, rotting logs, under rocks and sticks, and on green leaves.

Be sure to collect some of whatever material the insects were living in or on, such as green leaves, rotting wood, damp soil, sticks, etc., for your display.

⚠️ CAUTION Once you've collected a sufficient amount of insects, transfer them to the aquarium and the jars. Ask an adult to make several holes in the caps of the jars so air can reach the insects.

Remember that insects should be treated humanely. That is, don't keep them in an overly warm area in direct sunlight or in an overly cool air-conditioned room. Provide water and food for them and plan to release them back outdoors where you captured them.

Some questions you might place in front of this exhibit are:

Can you identify the insects seen here? Where would you expect to find each of them? (Answers vary.)

To collect insects for your permanent exhibit, you will need to find dead insects or order them from a science supply house. You can find dead insects on windowsills, between windows and screens, at the bottom of ceiling light covers, on basement floors, and so on.

To build your display, cover the bottom of the wooden or cardboard box with approximately 2 inches of corrugated cardboard. With large insects, simply push a pin carefully through their thoraxes, and insert the tip of the pin into the corrugated cardboard. With small or delicate insects, such as mosquitoes, glue them to the narrow end of a small triangular piece of paper, then push a pin through the wide end of the paper and into the cardboard (Fig. 6-4).

Figure 6-4

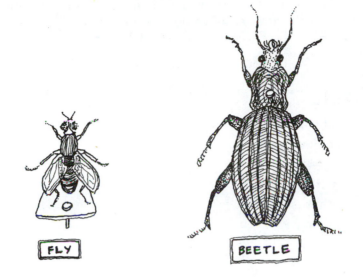

FLY

BEETLE

Particular care must be taken with insects that have fragile wings, such as butterflies, moths, dragonflies, and grasshoppers. Place fragile insects on a sheet of cardboard and carefully spread their wings so they are at right angles to their bodies. Hold the wings flat against the cardboard with small strips of paper and pins (Fig. 6-5). After about a week, the wings will be dry and the insect can be mounted to the corrugated cardboard along with the other insects.

Use a field guide to identify the insects if they are not familiar to you. A book on entomology will help you prepare some written material to accompany your dead insect exhibit.

To identify the insects being displayed, print or word process each insect's common and scientific name on a file card. Cut the file cards into small rectangles, then pin the cards beside the insects. For example, a card beside a butterfly might read: Monarch butterfly, Danaus plexippus.

Figure 6-5

Chicken skeleton

A chicken skeleton is perhaps the easiest skeleton to assemble because chicken bones are readily available. However, assembling the bones into a skeleton requires time and patience. This exhibit requires you to use boiling water, so an adult or parent **must** supervise this project.

Materials

➤ whole chicken[3]
➤ large cooking pot
➤ tongs
➤ heavy wire
➤ old toothbrush
➤ newspaper
➤ waxed paper
➤ modeling clay
➤ quick-drying glue
➤ illustration of a chicken skeleton[4]
➤ board, appx. 6 × 12 inches
➤ 2 dowels, appx. ½ inch in diameter
➤ drill
➤ measuring tape
➤ saw
➤ copy of Fig. 6-7
➤ table
➤ transparent tape

To prepare the skeleton, remove the meat from the bones. The best way to do this is to have an adult put the chicken in a pot of water and boil the water gently for approximately 2 hours. After approximately a half hour, ask your adult supervisor to cut off the chicken's head and remove it from the pot. The tongs can be used to hold the chicken's head above the water.

After 2 hours of cooking, the meat should be soft and easy to remove from the bones. Ask the adult helping you to drain off the water from the chicken. Cool the meat by filling the pot with cold water. You can then pull most of the meat off the bones with your

3 Purchase a mature chicken at a butcher shop. The bones of pullets and broilers are soft and not fully grown; they might disintegrate when cooked. Ask the butcher to dress the chicken (remove its innards) but leave the head and feet intact.

4 Books on poultry farming might be a good source for finding an illustration of a chicken skeleton.

fingers. The bones will come apart at the joints, so keep the bones from each leg and wing in separate piles. Any bones with meat on them might need to be placed back into boiling water for a few more minutes. If meat still sticks to the bone, hold the bone under running water and use an old toothbrush to rub it off. A piece of heavy wire is good for pushing meat out of small openings.

Once the bones are clean, place them on some newspaper and let them dry thoroughly. To assemble the skeleton, place the bones from each leg and foot on a sheet of waxed paper. Use clay to hold the bones in the proper position while you glue them together with a quick-drying glue. Do the same thing with each wing. These bones are shown assembled in Fig. 6-6a and 6-6b. Use an illustration that shows a chicken skeleton in detail to help you put things in the proper place.

Next, assemble the breast bone and connecting bones, such as the wishbone, that correspond to your clavicle, the shoulder blades, and coracoids. Can you find the hollow places where the wings join the rest of the body (Fig. 6-6c)?

Use the wire to assemble the vertebrae. Insert the wire through the hole in each vertebrae, which is where the spinal cord is located. There are usually 14 vertebrae in a chicken's neck. The first one is smaller than the rest and fits into a hole in the back of the chicken's skull bone. The seven tail vertebrae can be assembled in a similar way.

The 14 vertebrae of the pelvis are fused to the pelvic bones in mature chickens (Fig. 6-6d). The seven thoracic vertebrae have ribs attached to each side. Four other ribs extend upward from the breast bone. It will take great patience to glue the ribs in place.

You will need to build a stand for the skeleton before you put all the parts together. The board will serve as the base of the stand. Measure the length of the assembled leg bones before asking your adult supervisor to cut the first dowel to the proper length. Near one end of the wooden base, have an adult drill a hole into which you can insert the dowel upright and glue it in place. This dowel will support the lower side of the animal's fused pelvis. Place the second dowel just in front of the breast bone to support the bird's upright neck bones. Measure the length before asking your adult supervisor to cut the dowel, then have him or her drill another hole in the base to support this dowel. Glue this dowel in place as you did for the other one.

Glue the various parts together. Join the tail vertebrae to the pelvis. The wire through the tail can be placed into the pelvic vertebrae before the two regions are glued together. The body vertebrae and ribs can then be fixed to the front end of the pelvis. The breast bone and those glued to it can be connected next. Glue the rear end of the

Figure 6-6

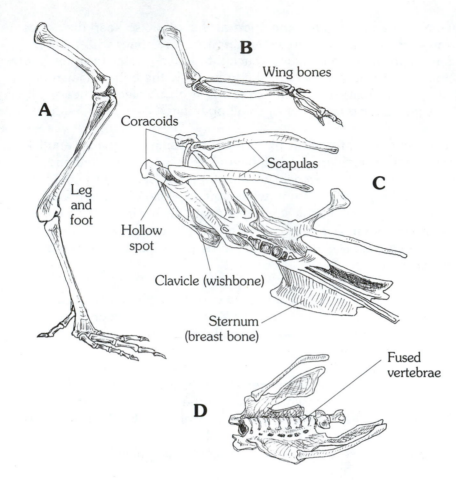

breast bone to the upright dowel supporting the pelvis. Glue the front end to the other dowel. Use wire to hold the bones in place as the glue dries.

Finally, attach the neck and head to the skeleton along with the legs and wings. Notice that there are round, hollow places into which the rounded ends of the femur and humerus bones fit. Barring a lack of patience, your chicken skeleton is now ready for display. Photocopy Fig. 6-7 and tape it to a wall or cardboard near the chicken skeleton.

Questions that might accompany the exhibit are:

How is this chicken skeleton similar to your own skeleton? (Answer: Many of the chicken's bones are similar, especially the leg and back bones, and it walks on two legs as I do.)

How is the chicken skeleton different from your skeleton? (Answer: Its wing bones are adapted for flying. Its bones are lighter. Its breast bone is quite different and so is its head.)

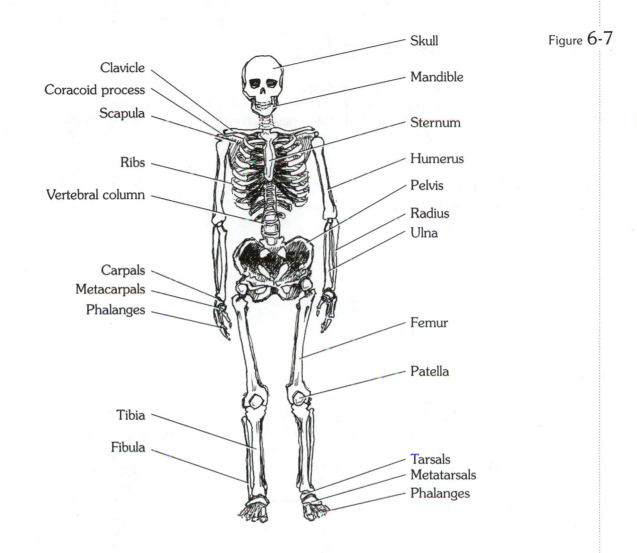

Figure 6-7

Skull

Clavicle
Coracoid process
Scapula

Mandible

Sternum

Ribs

Humerus

Pelvis

Vertebral column

Radius
Ulna

Carpals
Metacarpals
Phalanges

Femur

Patella

Tibia

Fibula

Tarsals
Metatarsals
Phalanges

Twigs and buds

In this exhibit, you can help museum visitors discover the source of a tree's new spring growth. Even though many trees do not have leaves in the winter, they do have new leaves waiting for spring. The new leaves are inside the buds.

Materials

➤ twigs taken from a number of different trees
➤ pruning clippers
➤ picture-type book of different trees
➤ masking tape
➤ pen and markers
➤ cloth or paper for the display
➤ magnifying glass
➤ pocket knife
➤ large vase with water

⚠ **CAUTION** Before you collect twigs from a tree, ask permission from the owners. Select live twigs that have buds like the one in Fig. 6-8. Cut several twigs from different types of trees with the pruning clippers. Place a piece of tape with the tree's name on each twig after you cut it. This way, you will be able to identify the twigs when you get back to your museum. If you don't know the names of the trees, use a picture-type book of trees to identify them.

Figure 6-8

Place the twigs with identifying labels on contrasting cloth or paper. If buds are plentiful, you might use a few of the twigs and buds as a hands-on exhibit. Invite visitors to examine a bud that you have opened by picking away a few of the brown scales from a terminal bud to expose the tiny leaves inside. Have a magnifying glass available so people can examine the opened buds. You will probably have to provide a new bud at least daily.

Invite visitors to use the magnifying glass to look at the leaf scars (Fig. 6-9) on the sides of the twigs. These scars were made by leaves that fell off in previous autumns. Call their attention to the dots that appear within the scars. These dots are the remains of the vessels that carried water, food, and minerals between the leaf and the stem of the twig.

Figure 6-9

Some of these scars look like "faces." Just for fun, you might like to color the "eyes" and "mouth" of one or two with markers to add a light touch to your exhibit.

Some buds will bloom during the winter if you put them in water and place them in a warm, sunny place. This is particularly true of maples and willows. Carefully cut off approximately ½ inch from the bottom of the twig each week. A clean cut allows water to enter the stem more easily. Those who visit your twigs exhibit might see that the terminal bud is where the twig grows longer in the spring.

Some questions you might ask visitors are:

Can you identify the trees from which these twigs were taken? (Answers will vary.)

Look closely at a leaf scar. It looks like this (provide a drawing). What makes the tiny dots inside the scar's outline? (Answer: Vessels that carry liquid to the leaves.)

Pinecones

Conifer bushes and trees are green all year. Their leaves, or needles, do not all drop off in autumn. The seeds of conifers are found not in fruits formed from flowers but in cones. If there are a number of different varieties of conifers in your area, such as white pine, sugar pine, pitch pine, spruce, and so on, you might collect the cones from the different species. The cones can serve as an attractive exhibit by themselves, particularly if you can show the seeds within or dropping from the cones.

You might also use the cones as part of a larger exhibit on the differences between gymnosperms (plants whose seeds are not formed in flowers) and angiosperms (flowering plants). The exhibit could include a small pine tree, one or two flowering plants, seeds within fruits (angiosperms), and seeds within cones (gymnosperms). Photographs of a variety of angiosperms and gymnosperms together with a brief discussion of their differences would enhance such an exhibit.

Seeds

When we talk about seeds, we have a vague picture of a seed, but seeds are a characteristic property of a plant. This exhibit will make it clear that the seeds of various plants can be very different.

Materials

- ➤ 12 each of various seeds
- ➤ self-adhesive labels
- ➤ glue
- ➤ 2 poster boards, one colored
- ➤ books that identify seeds
- ➤ illustrations or photographs of the life cycle of several seeds

Collect as many seeds as you can. Identify the seeds you collect by noting the plants, trees, or fruit from which they came. When you have collected enough for an exhibit, glue the seeds to the poster board. Leave approximately 3 to 4 inches between the rows of seeds. Stick labels above the seeds identifying their species so that those visiting your exhibit can identify them.

Create your own drawings or photographs to show how the seeds in at least one or two of the species fit into their life cycle. Use the other poster board as a display. If you grow pea plants in your garden, you could photograph or draw pictures of the pea plant's cycle. You might show pea seeds being planted, plants emerging from the soil, the flowers that blossom in the spring, the tiny pods that form in the pistils of the flowers, the pods that are picked for eating, and an open pod to reveal the seeds that can be stored, dried, and planted the following year.

Provide visitors with information on different types of seeds, such as the following:

Some seeds, such as bean, pea, squash, corn, pumpkin, tomato, and pepper seeds, are in the fruit that began as part of a flower. Many seeds can be found in the fruits we eat. Oranges, apples, cantaloupes, grapefruits, peaches, plums, grapes, and so on all contain seeds.

Other seeds, such as acorns, horse chestnuts, and beechnuts, come from the flowers of trees but are not covered by a fleshy fruit. In locust and catalpa trees, the seeds are inside long pods similar to, but larger than, pea pods. Maple trees produce seeds with wings that spin like helicopter blades as they fall from the tree. Pinecones contain seeds. If you bring the cones inside while they are still green, they will dry out and open, revealing the seeds within.

Wild plants produce seeds too. Some of them, milkweed and dandelion plants, for example, produce seeds with fluffy hairs. These seeds are easily carried by the wind, enabling the plants to spread over a wide area.

Crystals

Most people enjoy seeing crystals. In this exhibit, a solution of sodium thiosulfate (hypo), which is used as a fixer in processing photographs, is used to form the crystals. As water evaporates from the solution and the solution becomes saturated, crystals begin to form. The exhibit will have particular appeal in December as the holidays grow near.

Materials

➤ sodium thiosulfate crystals
➤ 8½ × 11 sheet of paper
➤ balance
➤ liquid measuring cup
➤ jar
➤ coffee stirrer or drinking straw
➤ petri dish
➤ transparent tape
➤ 8½ × 11 sheet of dark construction paper
➤ table
➤ food coloring
➤ twine

Place a sheet of paper on a balance and weigh out 50 grams of sodium thiosulfate crystals ($Na_2S_2O_3 \cdot 5H_2O$). Pour the crystals into the jar and add 50 milliliters of water. Use the coffee stirrer or drinking straw to stir the water until the crystals dissolve. Although sodium thiosulfate is not a particularly harmful or dangerous chemical, you should handle the solution with care—just as you would be careful not to breathe the vapors from ordinary household bleach. Protect your skin, eyes, and respiratory system whenever you use *any* type of chemical and always read the labels first.

Open the petri dish and place the dish and lid side by side on a dark sheet of paper taped to a table. Tape both the dish and the lid to the paper. Pour half the solution into the dish and the other half into the lid. Add a drop of food coloring to the dish. Leave the dish and the lid uncovered so that the water can evaporate. Do not leave the dish where any pets or small children can get into the solution.

When the solution becomes saturated, crystals will begin to form. The solutions should not be touched until all the water has evaporated. After the crystals have formed and no water remains, hang one or both of the dishes in a window. You can do this by taping a string to the edge of the dish or lid.

The information that accompanies this exhibit can be very simple:

DO NOT TOUCH THESE TWO DISHES! They contain water and sodium thiosulfate (hypo). One of them contains a drop of food coloring as well. As the water evaporates, crystals will eventually begin to form. How would you describe the crystals that form?

Rocks and minerals

If you are interested in rocks and minerals, you might prepare an exhibit for your museum that shows the difference between the two. If the region where you live has a variety of rocks, you could probably collect enough specimens to make a fairly extensive display.

Materials

➤ geologist's or stonemason's hammer
➤ safety glasses
➤ field guide for rocks and minerals
➤ materials to build display are varied, see the text

Use the geologist's or stonemason's hammer to chip away samples. Whenever you chip rocks, you should wear safety glasses to protect your eyes. A field guide for rocks and minerals can help you to identify samples that are not familiar to you.

There are several ways you can display your samples: behind glass on a slanted display board or in muffin baking tins or a clear plastic fishing tackle box. Choose the best method of displaying your collection based on the number, size, and weight of your samples.

To make a display that will be mounted on a board, put several drops of household cement on a specimen and press it onto the board. Use self-adhesive labels to identify each specimen. If a rock is too heavy to be glued in place, ask an adult to drill two holes in the board, tie thin wire around the rock, then slip the ends through the holes and twist together until the rock is held firmly in position.

Place smaller collections in a box divided into cylindrical or cubic sections, such as muffin tins or clear plastic fishing tackle boxes (see Fig. 6-10). To identify the samples, write numbers on the blank side of a file card. Use a paper punch to cut out the numbers. Place a tiny drop of white glue on a rock sample. Then, with the tip of a dampened finger or tweezers, place the number on the drop of glue. If you use a fishing tackle box, the opened top of the box can serve as a place for pasting on identifying numbered labels that match the numbers on the rock and mineral samples. With muffin tins, the labels can be stuck to the flat spaces between the cylindrical depressions.

Your display might also include non-rocks, that is, materials that resemble rocks but are not of natural origin, such as asphalt, concrete, melted glass, and bricks.

Figure 6-10

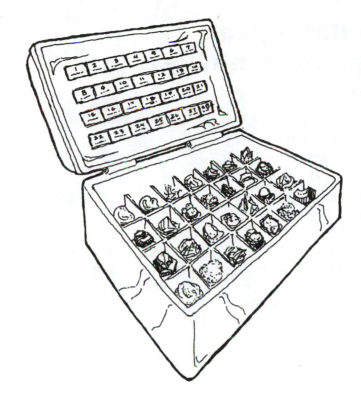

Some questions that might accompany your exhibit are:

Could any of these rocks be used to make statues or buildings? Which of these specimens are minerals?

Can you identify any non-rock rocks?

View through a stripped-down telescope
Materials

> 2 convex lenses (see text for further information)
> meterstick or yardstick
> lens holders
> modeling clay
> north-facing window (if you live above the Tropic of Cancer)
> copy of Fig. 6-11b

To build the simple telescope for this exhibit, you'll need two convex lenses. One lens should have a focal length of approximately 20 to 30 centimeters or more. The focal length of the other lens should be approximately 5 centimeters. A way to determine the focal length of a lens is discussed in "A convex lens and its images" in Part 3.

The objective lens—the lens closest to the object being viewed—should have the longer focal length and have as large a diameter as possible. The eyepiece lens, the lens you look through, should have the shorter focal length. The magnification depends on the ratio of the focal length of the objective lens to the focal length of the eyepiece lens.

Mount the objective lens on a meterstick or yardstick (Fig. 6-11a). If you can obtain lens holders from your school's science department, use them to support the lenses. Otherwise, you can mount the lenses in clay that can then be molded to the meterstick or yardstick.

Mount the eyepiece lens slightly beyond the focal point of the objective lens so that it can magnify the real image formed by the objective lens. Slowly move the eyepiece lens back and forth until you have the maximum magnification possible.

The best place for this exhibit at points north of the Tropic of Cancer is in front of a north-facing window with a view. Avoid locations where viewers might turn the telescope toward the sun. Find an object that can be clearly viewed through the telescope, and fix the telescope firmly in a position that "locks onto" the object.

Provide a copy of Fig. 6-11b for visitors along with the explanation and questions that follow:

Figure 6-11

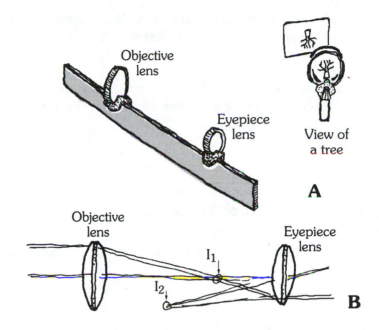

The drawing provided here shows how the lenses of a refractive telescope form a magnified image of an object that you can observe by looking through the eyepiece lens. After studying the diagram, look through the eyepiece. You will see a magnified, inverted image of (name of the object on which you have "locked" the telescope). *Never look at the sun through lenses of any kind, including the lens in your own eye. The sun can cause serious damage to your eyes.*

Estimate the magnification of the telescope. You can do this by keeping both eyes open as you look through the lenses. Compare the apparent height of (name of the object on which you have "locked" the telescope) with the height of its image as seen through the telescope. What is the magnifying power of this telescope? (Answer: Estimates will vary depending on the lenses used.)

View through a stripped-down compound microscope

The first microscopes consisted of a single lens with a very short focal length. These are known as *simple microscopes*. The microscopes found in biology laboratories today are called *compound microscopes* because they contain two lenses.

In a compound microscope, the lenses found in a telescope are reversed. The objective lens, which is closest to the object being viewed, has a shorter focal length than the eyepiece.

This exhibit shows how the lenses of a microscope form a magnified image of an object that you can observe by looking through the eyepiece lens.

Materials
> lens with focal length of 5 cm or less[5]
> plane mirror, appx. 2 to 3 inches on a side
> transparent tape
> 2 or 3 wooden blocks or bricks, large enough to support the mirror
> clear plastic wrap
> fine-tip marker
> scissors
> cardboard, appx. 3 inches on a side
> copy of Fig. 6-12b
> optional: ring stand and 2 C-clamps

A lens with a focal length of approximately 5 centimeters or less will be adequate for the objective lens in this exhibit. The eyepiece lens should have a focal length of approximately 10 centimeters. You will also need a plane mirror to reflect light, either natural or artificial, through the specimen and into the lenses (Fig. 6-12a).

Position the mirror at an angle, then use the blocks or bricks to support it and tape it into place. Cut a hole in the cardboard so that the mirror reflects light upward through the hole. Tape a clear piece of plastic over the hole. Use the marking pen to make a very small letter at the center of the hole. Choose a letter such as F, G, L, P, or R so that you will be able to tell when the image of the letter is upside down or turned right for left. Hold the objective lens (shorter focal length) over the letter. Slowly raise the lens until it is slightly

---

5 To find the focal length of a lens, see "A convex lens and its images," in Part 3.

Figure 6-12a

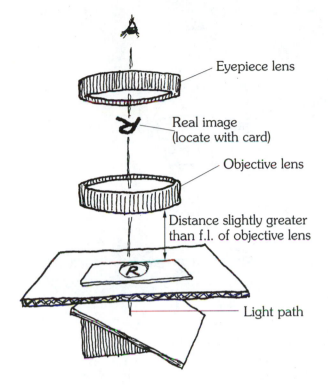

Eyepiece lens

Real image
(locate with card)

Objective lens

Distance slightly greater
than f.l. of objective lens

Light path

more than a focal length above the small letter. At this point, you should be able to see a magnified image of the letter that is inverted and turned right for left.

Use a ring stand and clamps or a sheet of cardboard held in place by bricks or blocks to support the objective lens at the required height. Hold the eyepiece lens, which has the longer focal length, above the first lens. It should be a little less than one focal length above the real image so that it will serve as a magnifying glass and produce an enlarged virtual image of the real image made by the objective lens. To find the best position for the eyepiece lens, move it up and down until you find the maximum magnification of the letter. Once you have found the best position for the eyepiece, use a ring stand and clamps or some other means to support it in a fixed position.

Provide a copy of Fig. 6-12b along with the following explanation and questions:

The drawing shows how the lenses of a microscope form a magnified image of an object that you can observe by looking through the eyepiece lens. After studying the diagram, look through the eyepiece. You will see a magnified inverted image of a (name of the letter on the plastic). Estimate the magnifying power of your microscope. You can do this by keeping both eyes open as you look through the lenses. Compare the height of the letter with the height of its image as seen through the microscope. What is the magnifying power of the microscope? (Answer: Estimates will vary depending on the lenses used.)

Figure 6-12b

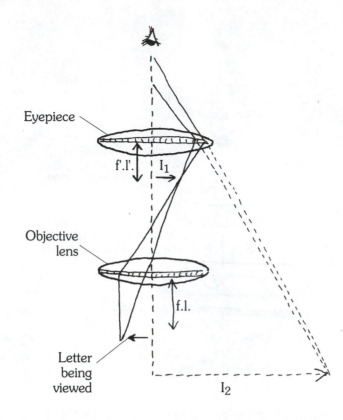

Eyepiece

f'.l'.   I₁

Objective
lens

f.l.

Letter
being
viewed

I₂

f.l. = Focal length of objective lens

f'.l'. = Focal length of eyepiece lens

I₁ = Real image formed by object

I₂ = Virtual image of real image
formed by eyepiece. (second image)

If you can borrow a real microscope from your school science department, you could add a second phase to your exhibit. The lenses used in the exhibit show how a microscope works but a real microscope with its better lenses enclosed in a tube provides viewers with an opportunity to see how something very tiny, such as a plant or animal cell, can be made clearly visible by magnification.

This part of the exhibit might be accompanied by a statement of the microscope's magnifying power (the product of magnifying powers found on the lenses, 10x × 20x for example), a brief indication of what is being viewed, and a question such as:

How does the construction of this microscope ensure that the lenses will be directly in line with one another?

A hallway rainbow

Rainbows appear in nature when sunlight is refracted and reflected by raindrops. The formation of a rainbow when sunlight illuminates falling raindrops is very complicated. However, the principles involved in making a rainbow can be demonstrated quite easily and visitors will enjoy viewing it.

Materials

➢ plane mirror, appx. 3 inches on a side
➢ shallow plastic dish
➢ water
➢ sunlight or artificial light
➢ white ceiling or wall
➢ table

Place the mirror in the dish and add some water. The water should lie in a beam of sunlight as shown in Fig. 6-13. If sunlight is not available, a strong artificial light source can be used.

Figure 6-13

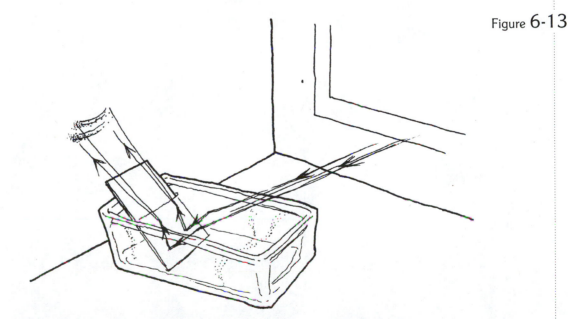

The "rainbow" produced when sunlight is refracted (bent) by the water and reflected by the mirror can be seen on a nearby white ceiling or wall. A patch of white light can also be seen, which is caused by light that is reflected by the part of the mirror that is not submerged.

If an artificial light source is used, choose a bright one. A bright light can be placed far enough from the dish so that the light rays reaching the mirror are, like rays of sunlight, very nearly parallel. If artificial light is used, the visibility of the rainbow will be enhanced if as little stray light as possible shines on the area around it.

The information accompanying this exhibit might read as follows:

The rainbow that you see on the (ceiling or wall) is formed by light reflected by a mirror partially submerged in water. As light passes from air to water and from water to air, it is refracted (bent). Because different colors in the white light, which is a combination of all the colors in the rainbow, are bent different amounts during refraction, the light spreads out into a rainbow.

What happens if you place your hand between the light and the water? (Answer: The rainbow disappears.) How can you explain the uncolored patch of white light that you see on the (ceiling or wall)? (Answer: It is due to the reflected light from the part of the mirror that is above the water.)

Bending light

This exhibit shows visitors that different colors of light are bent (refracted) differently.

Materials

- light box[6]
- prism
- flat-bottomed jar, at least 4 inches in diameter
- ruler
- water
- dimly lit area
- 2 sheets of 8½ × 11 white paper
- 2 sheets of 8½ × 11 black construction paper
- scissors
- transparent tape
- table

Tape the sheet of white paper to the tabletop on the left side of the light box as shown in Fig. 6-14. Put the prism on the paper and position so a single narrow beam of light is bent by the prism. (See "The law of reflection" in Part 3 for instructions on how to make a single narrow light beam like the one shown here.) Adjust the prism and you can produce a beautiful spectrum on the white paper.

Figure 6-14

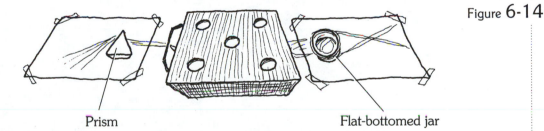

Prism   Flat-bottomed jar

On the right side of the light box, cover the opening in the box with a two-slit mask like the one used in "How a convex lens forms images," in Part 3.

Tape the other piece of white paper to the tabletop on the right side of the light box. Place the jar of water on the paper and position it. The jar of water behaves like a two-dimensional lens and converges the light "rays" that emerge from the box to form an image of a point of light from the bulb inside the box. However, because red light is refracted less than blue light, the blue light rays come together in front of the red rays.

6 To make the light box, see Part 3, "How a convex image lens forms images."

The information that accompanies the exhibit might read as follows:

A prism on the left shows how white light is bent (refracted) and broken into all the colors of the rainbow when it enters glass (plastic) at an angle. Which color is refracted the most by the prism? Which color is refracted the least?" (Answers: Violet (or blue) light is bent most; red is bent least.)

To the right of the light box, you see how a pair of light "rays" coming from a point on the light bulb inside the box are bent by a jar of water. The water acts like a lens; it brings the light rays together to form an image of the point of light on the white paper. Look closely at the two narrow light beams as they come together. Which color is bent the most? Which color is bent the least? Which colored light rays will meet first? What implications does this have for real lenses? (Answers: Blue light is bent more than the red light so blue rays will meet before red rays. Cheap lenses produce images with rainbowlike fringes. More expensive lenses are made by combining different types of glass so that the different colors of light converge at the same point.)

Breaking light into colors

In this exhibit, visitors will enjoy seeing light broken up and separated through a homemade spectroscope. A *spectroscope* is a device that breaks up and separates light into colors. When white light passes through a diffraction grating—the main component of one type of spectroscope—the entire visible spectrum can be seen. If the spectroscope is used to look at the light energy emitted when electricity is passed through a gas, the particular wavelengths (colors) characteristically produced by that gas will be separated by the spectroscope.

Materials

➤ lamp with fluorescent bulb, such as the type found in a study lamp or bathroom fixture
➤ mailing tube, appx. 6 inches long
➤ fixture for bulb
➤ 3 or 4 sheets of 8½ × 11 black construction paper
➤ transparent tape
➤ scissors
➤ diffraction grating[7]
➤ dimly lit area
➤ access to an electrical outlet

The spectroscope seen in Fig. 6-15a is made from a mailing tube lined with black construction paper to reduce the reflection of light inside the tube. Cut two semicircles to match the curvature of the tube from the black construction paper. Cover one end of the tube with the two semicircles. Leave a very narrow slit between the black semicircles so light can enter the tube. Tape the diffraction grating to the other end of the tube.

Turn the lamp so that the bulb is upright (Fig. 6-15b) and plug it into a nearby outlet. Although darkness is not essential, try to place the light in a dimly lighted area where stray light from other sources will not be confused with the light from the fluorescent bulb.

To see the spectrum from the fluorescent bulb, turn the spectroscope so that the narrow slit is the end of the tube closest to the light. The slit should be parallel to the long axis of the light bulb. Look through the diffraction grating at the other end of the tube. Then, if necessary, unfasten the grating and rotate it until you see the continuous spectrum spread out horizontally on both sides of the narrow beam of

---

7 A diffraction grating is a piece of plastic containing many parallel lines scratched into it. The most common is 13,400 lines per inch. You can purchase one from a hobby store, science supply house, or borrow it from a school science department.

Figure 6-15

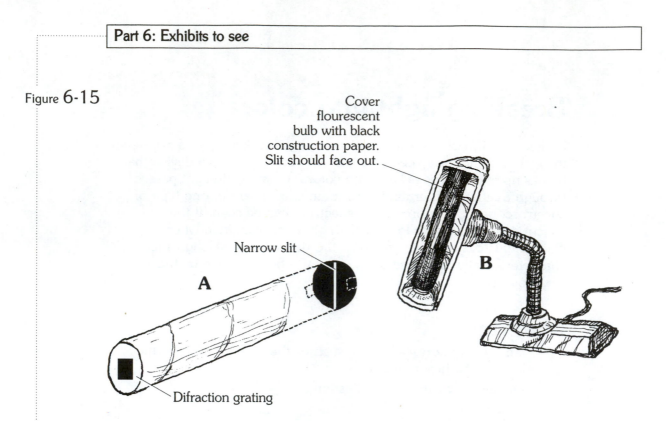

Cover
flourescent
bulb with black
construction paper.
Slit should face out.

Narrow slit

A

B

Difraction grating

light that enters the tube. You should also be able to see the characteristic spectral lines (colored lines) emitted by mercury vapor when it becomes energized by electricity.

Once the spectral lines can be clearly seen on each side of the grating, tape the spectroscope and light in place so they cannot be moved. The information presented to viewers can be quite simple:

Look through this spectroscope (tube). It can be used to analyze the light coming from the fluorescent light bulb. The spectroscope contains a diffraction grating that has 13,400 narrow openings per inch (or whatever yours is). When light passes through these narrow slits, it is separated into the wavelengths (colors) that make up the light. You can see the complete spectrum of colors produced by the frosted (fluorescent) part of the bulb to either side of the light itself. In addition, you will see the particular spectral lines (colors) emitted by the energized mercury vapor in the tube. These lines appear superimposed on the continuous spectrum. What are the colors of the spectral lines characteristic of mercury that you see here? (Answer: The green and violet lines can be seen quite clearly; the yellow line may not be visible.)

A hallway solar system

This exhibit, a scale model of the solar system, shows the sizes of the planets relative to the Sun and the vast distances that separate them.

Materials

➤ long hallway, such as one you might find in a school
➤ fishing line or kite twine
➤ thumbtacks
➤ transparent tape
➤ 3-×-5-inch file cards
➤ ball, appx. the size of a basketball or kickball
➤ net to hold ball (plastic net fruit sometimes comes in from the supermarket or a fishing net)
➤ ball bearings, marbles, or other spheres, appx. ⅟₁₆ inch to 1 inch
➤ tape measure
➤ books or encyclopedia that contains information on planets and the solar system

Use the book about planets to make up file cards containing information about each planet in our solar system: its size, its distance from the Sun, and, if you wish, its mass. A portion of the model—the Sun and Venus—is shown in Fig. 6-16. The sizes of the Sun and Venus are to scale; the distance between them is not.

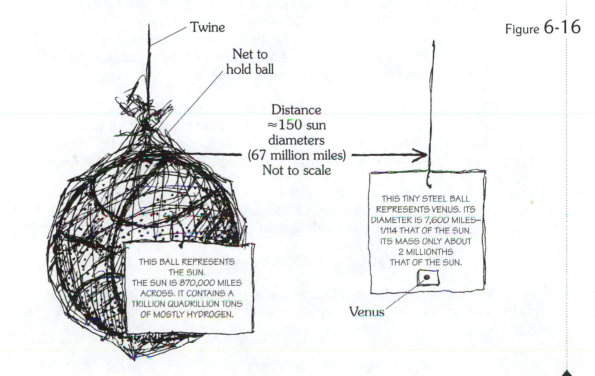

Twine

Net to hold ball

Distance ≈150 sun diameters (67 million miles) Not to scale

THIS BALL REPRESENTS THE SUN. THE SUN IS 870,000 MILES ACROSS. IT CONTAINS A TRILLION QUADRILLION TONS OF MOSTLY HYDROGEN.

THIS TINY STEEL BALL REPRESENTS VENUS. ITS DIAMETER IS 7,600 MILES— 1/114 THAT OF THE SUN. ITS MASS ONLY ABOUT 2 MILLIONTHS THAT OF THE SUN.

Venus

Figure 6-16

Hang the Sun and planets from a ceiling or molding along a wall with fishing line or twine and tape or thumbtacks. Attach a file card to the "Sun" indicating its size and, if you wish, its mass (2 quadrillion quadrillion kilograms). Because the planets are so small relative to the Sun, it is probably best to fasten the planets to a suspended file card. Table 6-1 provides the information you need to establish the scaled sizes of the Sun and planets and the distances of the planets from the Sun.

Table 6-1

The Sizes, Distances, and Relative Sizes and Distances of the Sun and Planets that Make Up the Solar System

Object	Diameter (miles × 1,000)	Relative diameter (Earth = 1.0)	Radius of orbit (miles × 1,000,000)	Relative radius of orbit (Earth = 1.0)
Sun	870	108	–	–
Mercury	3.0	0.38	36	0.39
Venus	7.6	0.95	67	0.72
Earth	8.0	1.0	93	1.0
Mars	4.2	0.53	141	1.52
Jupiter	90	11.3	480	5.2
Saturn	75	9.4	880	9.5
Uranus	33	4.1	1,790	19.2
Neptune	31	3.9	2,800	30.1
Pluto	1.6	0.2	3,660	39.4

If you use a basketball, which is 9.5 inches in diameter, to represent the Sun, the object used to represent Earth will be only 0.09 inch across because 9.5/108 ≈ 0.09. (The symbol ≈ means "approximately equal to.") There is no need to find something exactly 0.09 inch in diameter. A ⅛-inch (0.125-inch) ball bearing will illustrate that Earth is tiny compared to the Sun.

Because Earth is 93 million miles from the Sun and the Sun's diameter is 0.87 million miles, the tiny object representing Earth must be placed more than 100 basketball diameters from the center of the "Sun" because 93/0.87 = 107, and 107 × 9.5 inches ≈ 1016 inches.

Since there are 12 inches in a foot and 3 feet in a yard, the separation of Sun and Earth in your model should be

1,016 in./12 in./ft ≈ 85 feet; or 85 ft/3 ft/yd ≈ 28 yards.

Between the Earth and Sun lie the orbits of the planets Mercury and Venus. How far should each of them be from the Sun in your model?

Since the orbit of Mars has a radius that is 1.52 times as large as Earth's, Mars will have to be placed approximately 42 yards (126 ft) from the basketball. Will the orbit of Mars "fit" into your exhibit area?

The object representing Jupiter can be approximately 1 inch in diameter since its diameter is approximately $\frac{1}{10}$ that of the Sun and 11.3 times that of the Earth (11.3 × 0.09 in. ≈ 1.0 in.). However, it must be placed nearly 150 yards from the basketball because 5.2 × 28 yd = 146 yd. It's highly unlikely that Jupiter will fit in your exhibit area. The other planets, Saturn at 265 yards, Uranus at 540 yards, Neptune at 840 yards, and Pluto at 1100 yards or 0.625 miles, will have to be placed outside.

In fact, you might want to limit your exhibit to whatever will fit into the space that is available to you and simply explain where the other planets would be located if space were available. Of course, you could reduce the scale by using something such as a tennis ball, which has a diameter of approximately 2.5 inches, to represent the Sun. However, the Earth on that scale would then be less than 0.025 inch.

Identifying trees

Trees can be identified by studying their leaves and their bark. In this exhibit, leaf rubbings, pressed leaves, and bark from different trees make a very attractive art and science exhibit.

Materials

➤ leaves from various trees
➤ crayons or soft-lead pencil
➤ 8½ × 11 white paper, enough for each leaf
➤ countertop or table
➤ transparent tape
➤ self-adhesive labels
➤ book on plants and trees
➤ 2, 8½ × 11 sheets of thin cardboard
➤ several heavy books

Rather heavy rigid lines form the "skeleton" of a leaf (Fig. 6-17). This skeleton of veins carries water and food between the plant's stem and the leaves and provides a framework for the leaf's tissue. The structure of the veins within a leaf form a pattern that is characteristic of the type of tree it comes from.

Figure 6-17

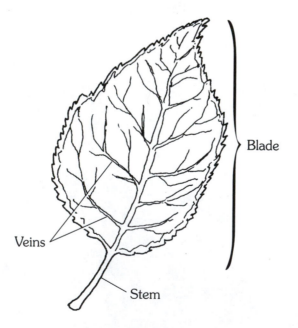

Blade

Veins

Stem

To make a leaf rubbing, place a leaf upside down on a table or counter. Place a piece of white paper over the leaf. Rub a crayon or a soft-lead pencil carefully back and forth over the paper until the outline of the leaf's veins appear. Do a leaf rubbing for each leaf you've collected. These leaf rubbings will be exhibited together with a collection of pressed leaves from a variety of trees.

Leaves will curl up as they dry, so they must be pressed. To press leaves, fasten a leaf to a sheet of paper with tape. If there is room, put several leaves on each sheet. Tape a printed label to the paper that identifies each leaf. When all the leaves in your collection have been taped to sheets of paper, place the sheets on top of one another on a piece of cardboard. Cover the sheets with a second sheet of cardboard to make a leaf "sandwich." Finally, place several heavy books on top of the sandwich and leave it for several weeks. As the leaves dry, they will be pressed flat and be ready for your exhibit (Fig. 6-18).

Figure 6-18

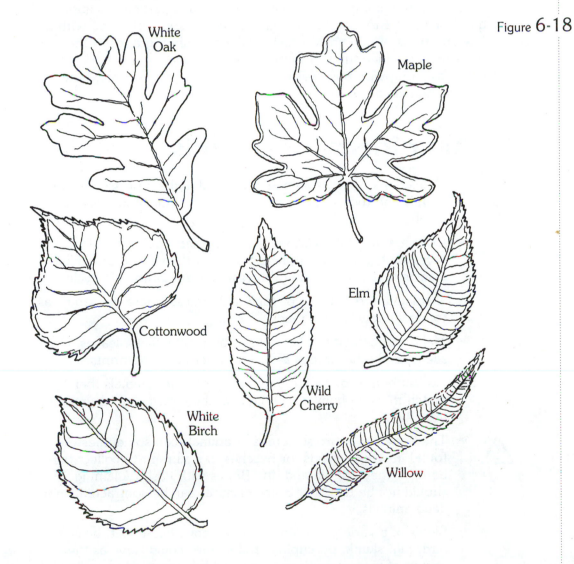

White Oak

Maple

Cottonwood

Elm

Wild Cherry

White Birch

Willow

During the fall, you might like to collect beautiful red, yellow, and orange leaves. Place the leaves between sheets of waxed paper or plastic and press them with a pile of books.

In addition to their leaves, trees can be identified by their bark. To make a bark rubbing, have someone stand on one side of a tree and reach around the trunk to hold a sheet of white paper firmly against the bark on the other side. Move a crayon or a soft-lead pencil back and forth across the paper to make a rubbing of the bark. The bark rubbings can then be exhibited beside the corresponding leaf rubbings.

The information you provide users and your display could be presented in many ways, so I have not provided particular sample questions and answers. You could just display your collection with a few questions or you could provide full color photographs of the trees that provided the leaf rubbings, pressed leaves, and bark rubbings along with poster-size illustrations of leaf anatomy, how leaves change colors, etc.

Other ideas for exhibits

➤ Collections, such as animal horns and antlers, pressed flowers, metals and their ores, and polished gems, make interesting displays.

➤ Collect and exhibit various types of insect cocoons and crysalids together with photographs or drawings of the adult insects that emerge from this resting stage of the life cycle.

➤ Display different types of sand and discuss where the sand was found or how sand is made.

➤ Make and exhibit plaster casts of bones, feathers, leaves, tree seeds, and other things as well as tracks and footprints.

➤ Collect bones, or pictures of bones, of other animals that match those in humans. Of course, the bones may be greatly modified.

➤ The bones or entire skeletons of animals can sometimes be found in woods, fields, or beaches. It's all right to collect these bones if they are old and dry. Bones with flesh remaining should not be touched. Some diseases can be contracted from dead animals.

➤ Skulls of a variety of animals—deer, cow, horse, cat, beaver, bird, pig, skunk, porcupine, and so on—could serve as the source of many questions that could be presented in an exhibit.

➤ Fossils, together with photographs and descriptions of the times when these plants or animals inhabited the earth, can make a very interesting exhibit. Fossils are often difficult to find, however, and you should be careful not to disturb any that might offer clues about early life on earth. If you are interested in making a fossil exhibit, consult someone at a nearby university or large museum and ask for guidance.

➤ Take photographs of various types of cloud formations using a variety of exposures and filters with both black and white and color film. Try to include cumulus, cirrus, stratus, and more subtle forms of clouds such as cirrocumulus, cirrostratus, and stratocumulus. Use printed material or audio tape to explain how clouds form, the characteristics of different types of clouds, and the weather that various cloud formations indicate.

➤ Photographs of trees, preferably in color, could make a nice addition to the exhibit of leaves and leaf and bark rubbings described above. Photographs of different species of trees taken at various times of the year could make an interesting exhibit by itself. The photographs could be accompanied by an explanation of where each specie can be found, its use and economic importance, and any other interesting information. Information about maple trees, their sap, and the process of making maple syrup could be the basis of an exhibit that might include photographs of the collection and processing of the sap as well as the trees themselves in their spectacular autumn colors.

➤ Prepare an exhibit based on photographs revealing the characteristic shapes of different species of trees.

➤ Photographs of different flowers could make a beautiful exhibit or use a series of photographs to show the life cycle of a flowering plant. Spice it up with real flowers in pots or vases along with samples of seeds, including seeds within a fruit that has been cut open.

➤ Place a pair of radiometers in a lighted area. Provide a means of covering one so that the intensity of the light striking the spinning vanes is greatly reduced to discover how the rate at which the radiometer turns is affected by light intensity.

➤ Prepare an exhibit using pH paper to measure the acidity of various liquids.

➤ Use various magnets and iron filings to map magnetic field lines.

➤ Design a demonstration for visitors to measure the extent of their peripheral vision.

➤ Prepare a demonstration to show some of the properties of polarized light.

➤ Develop a way to show how changing light intensity affects the size of the pupils in one's eyes.

➢ Design a demonstration to show how the intensity of light or sound diminishes as the distance increases. (For a small source, doubling the distance reduces intensity to ¼.)

➢ Use an aquarium and a laser (or suitable substitute) to show the critical angle for light entering air from water. At the critical angle, all the light is reflected back into the water.

➢ Develop an exhibit that shows how a camera works. As a sequel, design an exhibit to show how film is developed.

➢ Many children are fascinated by dinosaurs. Invite them to draw their favorite dinosaurs and submit the drawings to you. You could then display their work in an exhibit together with pictures of dinosaurs and dinosaur skeletons that you can find in various books and magazines. Include printed material in the exhibit. The subject matter will encourage them to read. Use large print and keep the words and sentences short. Before you place the printed matter in the exhibit, show it to a primary-grade teacher. He or she will be able to suggest changes that might make the reading level more appropriate for young children.

➢ Design activities to encourage people to exercise their powers of imagination. Invite people to invent their own imaginary animals. To communicate the appearance of their fantasy animal to others, ask them to submit drawings that you will display. After all the drawings are on exhibit, you might add a number to each drawing. You could then sponsor a contest by inviting visitors who come to the exhibit to vote for their favorite fantasy animal. Attach a pen or pencil by string to a slotted box into which the ballots can be placed. Small sheets of paper torn from a pad fixed to the box could serve as ballots. A blue ribbon could be attached to the winning drawing after the voting deadline has past.

➢ As a follow-up exhibit or as an alternate exhibit to fantasy animals, ask visitors to draw *and* describe the adaptations of an imaginary animal destined to live in a wet climate. Hold a contest involving the imaginary animals best suited to life in a dry climate, a cold climate, and a hot climate. Contest winners could be selected by a panel of science teachers rather than by voting. The reason for a panel of "experts" is that contestants must take into account the consequences of the climate on their imaginary animals when they describe its adaptations. For example, an animal designed for a hot climate must have a large surface area and other means of shedding heat, such as sweat glands.

Metric
conversions

Length
1 inch (in) = 2.54 centimeters (cm)
1 foot (ft) = 30 cm
1 yard (yd) = 0.90 meters (m)
1 mile (mi) = 1.6 kilometers (km)

Volume
1 teaspoon (tsp) = 5 milliliters (ml)
1 tablespoon (tbsp) = 15 ml
1 fluid ounce (fl oz) = 30 ml
1 cup (c) = 0.24 liters (l)
1 pint (pt) = 0.47 l
1 quart (qt) = 0.95 l
1 gallon (gal) = 3.80 l

Mass
1 ounce (oz) = 28.00 grams (g)
1 pound (lb) = 0.45 kilograms (kg)

Temperature
32 degrees Fahrenheit (F) = 0 degrees Celsius (C)
212 degrees F = 100 degrees C

Resources

Carolina Biological Supply Co.
2700 York Rd.
Burlington, NC 27215
(910) 584-0381

Central Scientific Co. (CENCO)
3300 CENCO Pkwy.
Franklin Park, IL 60131
(800) 262-3626

Connecticut Valley Biological
Supply Co., Inc.
82 Valley Rd., Box 326
Southampton, MA 01073
(800) 628-7748

Delta Education
P.O. Box 915
Hudson, NH 03051-0915
(800) 258-1302

Edmund Scientific Co.
101 East Gloucester Pk.
Barrington, NJ 08007
(609) 573-6270

Fisher Scientific Co.
485 S. Frontage Rd.
Burr Ridge, IL 60521
(800) 955-1177

Frey Scientific Co.
905 Hickory Ln.
Mansfield, OH 44905
(800) 225-3739

Nasco Science
901 Janesville Rd.
Fort Atkinson, WI 53538-0901
(800) 558-9595

Schoolmasters Science
745 State Circle
P.O. Box 1941
Ann Arbor, MI 48106
(313) 761-5072

Science Kit & Boreal Laboratories
777 East Park Dr.
Tonawanda, NY 14150
(800) 828-7777

Wards Natural Science, Inc.
5100 West Henrietta Rd.
P.O. Box 92912
Rochester, NY 14692-9012
(800) 962-2660

Bibliography

Brown, Vinson. *Building Your Own Nature Museum: For Study and Pleasure*. 1984. New York: Arco.

Gardner, Robert. *Experimenting with Illusions*. 1990. New York: Watts.

_____. *Experimenting with Inventions*. 1990. New York: Watts.

_____. *Investigate and Discover Forces and Machines*. 1991. Englewood Cliffs, N.J.: Messner.

_____. *Robert Gardner's Favorite Science Experiments*. 1992. New York: Watts.

_____. *Science Projects about Electricity and Magnetism*. 1994. Hillside, N.J.: Enslow.

Gardner, Robert and Webster, David. 1976. *Shadow Science*. New York: Doubleday.

The Exploratorium Science Snackbook. 1991. San Francisco: The Exploratorium.

How to Make a Chicken Skeleton. 1965. Elementary Science Study. Watertown, Mass.: Elementary Science Study.

Teacher's Guide for Bones. 1968. Elementary Science Study, St. Louis: Webster Division, McGraw-Hill.

Teacher's Guide for Microgardening. 1965. Elementary Science Study. Watertown, Mass.: Educational Services Incorporated.

Tocci, Salvatore. *How to Do a Science Fair Project*. 1986. New York: Watts.

Webster, David. *Brain Boosters*. 1966. Garden City, N.Y.: The Natural History press.

_____. *How to Do a Science Project*. 1974. New York: Watts.

_____. *More Brain Boosters*. 1966. Garden City, N.Y.: The Natural History Press.

_____ . *Photo Fun: An Idea Book for Shutterbugs*. 1973. New York: Watts.

Index

Illustration page numbers are in **boldface**.

About the author

Robert Gardner is a former chairman of the science department at Salisbury School in Connecticut where he taught physics, chemistry, biology, and physical science. He was also a staff member of the Elementary Science Study and the Physical Science Group at the Education Development Center in Newton, Massachusetts where he developed science curriculum materials for both elementary and secondary schools.

Gardner is the author of more than 50 books for young people, including *Kitchen Chemistry*, *The Whale Watchers' Guide*, *Ideas for Science Projects*, *Famous Experiments You Can Do*, *Crime Lab 101*, *Experimenting with Science in Sports*, and many others.

Gardner retired from teaching in 1989 to devote his attention to writing full time and doing volunteer work in Eastham, Massachusetts where he now lives with his wife, Natalie.